PRIMA LATINA

An Introduction to Christian Latin

2nd Edition

TEACHER MANUAL

By Leigh Lowe

CLASSICAL TRIVIUM CORE SERIES

Your Next Latin Program
Latina Christiana I
by Cheryl Lowe

Once you complete *Prima Latina*, the next recommended course is *Latina Christiana I.*

Prima Latina: Teacher Manual
by Leigh Lowe

Published by:

Memoria Press
www.MemoriaPress.com

Second Edition 2003
First Edition 2002
ISBN #: 1-930953-52-6

Prima Latina (A Latin precursor for young children)

Prima Latina is a preparatory course for Cheryl Lowe's *Latina Christiana*. It is intended for teachers with no background in Latin and was developed for children in first through fourth grade. The course was designed for students who are still becoming familiar with English grammar but are competent readers. Its goal is to teach and reinforce an understanding of the basic parts of speech while introducing Latin vocabulary and grammar. This course provides a solid foundation in grammar before moving on to more advanced language and Latin skills. *Prima Latina* is an ideal precursor to *Latina Christiana*, as the vocabulary and format are taken directly from the *Latina Christiana I* text. The book is accompanied by an audio CD for pronunciation guidance. *Latina Christiana I Flash Cards* are an ideal study aid for *Prima Latina* and a great investment for the parent or teacher who intends to use *Latina Christiana I* and *II* as successor courses.

A great new study aid is now available from Memoria Press, *Prima Latina Instructional Videos* taught by Leigh Lowe. Call your favorite curriculum provider or visit www.MemoriaPress.com for information on these videos and other great Memoria Press books.

Prima Latina uses the clear and systematic format developed in *Latina Christiana* to introduce Latin to young students. The course teaches students seven parts of speech, 125 Latin vocabulary words, numbers 1 through 10, basic constellations, and simple introductions to tenses, derivatives, conjugations, and declensions. Each of the 25 new lessons consists of a new grammar skill, five vocabulary words that correspond with the lesson, a practical Latin phrase, and one line of a prayer that is learned in totality by the end of the chapter. The exercises that accompany each lesson are thorough and provide constant review of materials learned throughout the course. The book includes five review lessons, five tests, an appendix, and an answer key.

I hope that *Prima Latina* inspires in your child a love of the Latin language and a foundation that proves helpful in many areas of study. I wish you the best of luck as you begin what will hopefully be an enjoyable and fruitful study of Latin.

Ora et Labora,

Leigh Lowe

Leigh Lowe

gr 4   greek roots
gr 5   latin roots
gr 6   Prima Latina
gr 7   Getting started ...
gr 8   Latina I
gr 9   Greek
gr 10   Latina II
gr 11   Wheelocks? Spanish?
gr 12   "   "

Pronunciation Rules

The Alphabet

The Latin alphabet has no "w". Words with "y" are of Greek origin.

Vowels

In Christian Latin vowels are usually long.

Vowel	Long	Example
a	'father' (ah)	ambulo
e	'they' (ay)	deus
i	'machine' (ee)	via
o	'no' (oh)	toga
u	'rule' (oo)	luna

Sometimes the vowels **e** and **i** tend toward the short vowel sounds ('Ed','it') as in 'mensa' and 'et'.

Diphthongs and digraphs

Digraph	Pronunciation	Example
ae	like *e* in 'they' (ay)	caelum
oe	like *e* in 'they' (ay)	proelium

Diphthong		
au	like ou in cow (ow)	laudo, nauta

Consonants

Most of the consonants are pronounced as in English, with the following exceptions.

Consonant	Pronunciation	Examples
c	soft before *e, i, ae, oe,* like *ch* in 'charity'	decem, caelum
c	hard before other letters, like *c* in 'cut'	clamo, corona
g	soft before *e, i, ae, oe* like *g* in 'germ'	regina, gemini
g	hard before other letters like *g* in 'go'	toga, navigo
gn	like *gn* in 'lasagne'	pugno
j	like *y* in 'yet'	Jesus, judico
s	like *s* in 'sing' (never like *z*)	tres, mensa
sc	like sh	discipulus
t	like *tsee,* when followed by *i* and a vowel	etiam

Table Of Contents

Grammar Overview

This grammar overview is designed for the teacher who has no background in Latin. It is not necessary to understand it fully. Read carefully and then go on to the teacher guidelines. The content of this section will become clear as you teach the course.

Ancient languages such as Latin and Greek are highly **inflected.** This means that the relationship between words (syntax) is shown by changing the endings of the words. In modern languages like English, which have little inflection, the relationship between words is shown by **word order and prepositions.**

Cases of Nouns

In English we can change the end of a noun to make it plural or possessive. So *girl* can also be written *girls, girl's or girls'.* In pronouns we use different forms, such as *he* or *him,* for subject and object. These are examples of **inflection** in English. In Latin there is much more inflection. The endings of nouns change depending on their **function** in the sentence. The different **functions** a noun can perform in a sentence are called **cases.**

> **Nominative case:** nouns that are subjects or predicate nouns.
> **Genitive case:** nouns that are possessive.
> **Dative case:** nouns that are indirect objects.
> **Accusative case:** nouns that are direct objects / prep. ob.
> **Ablative case:** nouns that are prepositional objects.

Declensions

Writing a noun with all of its case endings in both the singular and plural is called DECLINING a noun. The DECLENSION of puella (girl) in Latin is:

	Singular	Plural
Nom.	puella *(girl)*	puellae *(girls)*
Gen.	puellae *(of the girl / girl's)*	puellarum *(of the girls / girls')*
Dat.	puellae *(to or for the girl)*	puellis *(to or for the girls)*
Acc.	puellam *(girl)*	puellas *(girls)*
Abl.	puella *(by, with, or from the girl)*	puellis *(by, with, or from the girls)*

In Latin there are **FIVE DECLENSIONS -** groups of nouns that have the same or similar case endings. The declension above is the FIRST DECLENSION. Students will learn two declensions in this book and will learn the next three declensions in Book II.

Latin Word Order

Word order is very important in English because it indicates the function of the noun. The subject comes first in the sentence.

The girl sees the queen	The queen sees the girl
sub. *d.o.*	*sub.* *d.o.*

In Latin the subject and direct object are indicated by the case endings of the nouns, **not the order of the words.** Both of the Latin sentences below mean the same thing even though the word order is different.

<table>
<tr><td>Puella regin<u>am</u> videt</td><td>Regin<u>am</u> puella videt</td></tr>
<tr><td>Girl   queen   sees</td><td>Queen   girl   sees</td></tr>
<tr><td>S.   D.O.</td><td>D.O.   S.</td></tr>
</table>

Both translate: *The girl sees the queen.* The direct object, *reginam* (queen), is signaled by the accusative ending *am*, not by its position following the subject and verb.

Verbs

In Latin, the different forms of verbs are constructed by inflection, adding different endings to the verbs rather than by adding helping verbs as in English.

voco	I call
vocabo	I will call
vocabam	I was calling

There are six tenses of verbs in Latin and English. This year we will learn three tenses.

Writing a verb with its endings which indicate *person, number, tense, etc.* is called conjugating a verb. There are four groups of verbs that have the same or similar endings and they are called conjugations. We will learn the first two CONJUGATIONS this year. Here is the **First Conjugation**.

Present Tense

	Singular		Plural	
1st Person	voco	*I call*	vocamus	*we call*
2nd Person	vocas	*you call*	vocatis	*you call*
3rd Person	vocat	*he, she, it calls*	vocant	*they call*

Student Goals for *Prima Latina*

1. Learn basic Latin alphabet and pronunciation of vowels and consonant sounds.

2. Pronounce, spell and translate approximately 125 Latin words.

3. Learn 25 practical Latin expressions and 4 prayers in full.

4. Learn numbers 1 through 10.

5. Learn names of popular constellations.

6. Understand concept of derivatives, English words that are derived from Latin.

7. Grammar
   A. Learn to identify basic parts of speech including verbs, nouns, prepositions, pronouns, adjectives, adverbs, and conjunctions.
   B. Recognize that conjugating is associated with verbs.
   C. Recognize that declining is associated with nouns.
   D. Memorize 1st declension noun endings.
   E. Memorize 1st conjugation verb endings.

General Teaching Guidelines

Prima Latina is a preparatory course for Cheryl Lowe's *Latina Christiana* series. It is intended for teachers with no background in Latin and was developed for children in first through fourth grade. The course was designed for students who are still becoming familiar with English grammar and reinforces understanding of the basic parts of speech before moving on to more advanced language and Latin skills. The course requires high teacher involvement for younger students or beginning readers. Prima Latina is a course that may be repeated, with extra skills like songs and derivatives available for students as they become more comfortable with the core objectives.

Prima Latina Lessons are comprised of the following five parts:

Lesson

Each lesson is plainly laid out in the student book. Many of the lessons introduce or reinforce English parts of speech. Each lesson gives definitions and examples for each new concept. It is always advantageous to go over new ideas several times. A teacher can supplement examples and let the student think up examples of her own.

Vocabulary

The vocabulary list directly corresponds to each week's lesson. There are usually five words in each lesson. First listen to the vocabulary words on the CD. There is time allowed for students to repeat what they have heard while listening. Have students follow along in their workbook, pointing to each word spoken on the CD. Then, turn off the CD and practice saying each word, paying particular attention to pronunciation. Discuss each word in relation to the lesson of the week. Talk about each word's meaning, and spelling. By making a big deal about each vocabulary word and giving it considerable attention, the child has more opportunities to grasp something that makes that word meaningful and consequently learns the word more permanently. Use the Vocabulary Drill Forms to have the child write and translate the vocabulary words five times as instructed in the Write and Learn section of the exercises for each lesson. For advanced students, derivatives are available for each lesson. Be sure your child is very comfortable with the difference between derivatives and definitions before introducing these into your lessons. Derivatives can be extraordinarily helpful, but they can also confuse a novice Latin student. A complete lesson on derivatives is available in Lesson 8.

Practical Latin

The Latin sayings are available each week to give a child a fun way to integrate his Latin education into daily life. By teaching a child how to say words and expressions he already uses in an exciting new way, he develops pride and a curiosity which drives further study. Have the child use the Practical Latin lessons every day to implant them into memory. *It is important to note that the grammatical rules of Latin have been simplified in the Prima Latina lessons to introduce students to the language. The Latin Sayings may at times appear to contradict lessons taught in the book as they are subject to more advanced grammatical rules.*

Latin Prayers

The Latin Prayers are broken up each week as one line of four complete prayers, The Sanctus, The Table Blessing, The Pater Noster (Our Father or Lord's Prayer), and The Doxology. By the end of each chapter, the child has learned the entire prayer line by line and should be able to recite it from memory in its totality. Have the child recite what he knows of the prayer five times everyday. It is also helpful to have the child write as much as he knows of each prayer as a memory aid. *It is important to note that the grammatical rules of Latin have been simplified in the Prima Latina lessons to introduce students to the language. The Latin Prayers may at appear to contradict defy lessons taught in the book as they are subject to more advanced grammatical rules.*

Exercises Overview

Each lesson includes exercises organized into the following parts:

Review Exercises: These are questions that help a child retain information previously learned in the course. The questions pull information from all parts of earlier lessons. See if a child can answer the questions without looking up the information. A child may refer back to the earlier lesson if need be. The child may answer the questions directly in his work book.

Lesson-Specific Questions: These questions pull the most important information from each lesson. A child can refer back to the lesson to answer the questions if necessary. The child may answer the questions directly in his workbook if the teacher approves.

Translate: Translating gives the child practice learning the new Latin word and its English meaning. The child can write the answers to the translation section in his workbook. The Write and Learn section of the Exercises provides supplemental practice.

Speaking Latin: The student should say each vocabulary word correctly five times. You can use the audio CD to confirm correct pronunciation.

Write and Learn: Use space in the exercises to have the student write each vocabulary word as three times. A reproducible Drill Form is provided in the teacher manual for extra vocabulary & grammar practice.

Fun Practice: Fun practice provides an entertaining exercise to reinforce the lesson of the week. These exercises can generally be done directly in the workbook.

Latin Songs: In each review lesson all or part of a Latin song is available for review. Songs are a great way to get children excited about Latin. Additional songs are available on the Lingua Angelica CD, which is a supplement to Prima Latina.

Supplements

**Audio CD
The audio CD provides the vocabulary words, Practical Latin, and Latin Prayers for each lesson. It is organized to serve as an accompaniment to the student text and is to be used with the Vocabulary Drill Forms. As a bonus, it includes the songs from Lingua Angelica that are introduced in Prima Latina.

**Prima Latina Instructional Video
If you would like extra help learning or teaching Latin, these instructional videos feature Leigh Lowe teaching the entire _Prima Latina_ course.

**Flash Cards
Because the vocabulary and many of the Practical Latin sayings are pulled directly from the _Latina Christiana I_ text, the _Latina I Flashcards_ are a wonderful aid for the _Prima Latina_ program. There are some words in the _Latina I Flashcard_ set that are not used in _Prima Latina_, but the cards make a great investment if _Latina I_ will be your next step in Latin education. The additional words can also provide extra material for the advanced student.

**Lingua Angelica
Lingua Angelica is a wonderful supplement to all of the Memoria Press Latin programs. Each review lesson in Prima Latina introduces a song from the _Lingua Angelica CD_. Students can learn these songs and can simply listen to the other beautiful Latin hymns and identify familiar words in the verses. You will soon find that young students love the _Lingua Angelica_ songs.

A Sample Lesson Plan

Each *Prima Latina* lesson is designed to be completed weekly. This sample lesson is intended as a once per week class or a daily course that meets four to five times per week. It simply outlines a suggested breakdown of the components and can be adjusted to meet the needs of your particular teaching environment.

1. Begin Class with a Practical Latin greeting—for example, "Salve" or "Quid Agis?" Have the students respond appropriately. As you learn more Practical Latin sayings, incorporate them accordingly into your classes.

2. Review previously learned material by oral question-and-answer session, checking Review Exercises, and/or a short written quiz.

3. Teach complete lesson as given in the text. Pronounce and discuss each vocabulary word, the Practical Latin Saying, and the Latin Prayers. Talk about the English derivatives of the words. Each week prayer lines accumulate. Work on adding the new line to what students already know.

4. Drill with CD exercises and complete Speaking Latin and Write and Learn Exercises.

5. Complete Lesson-Specific Questions and Translate Exercises.

6. Review all four parts of lesson, complete Fun Practice Exercise, drill with flashcards, and play review games if time allows.

Nomen:_____

A. Answer the following questions in English.

1. What are ACTION words called? _____

2. How many vowels are there? _____

3. What letter is missing from the Latin alphabet? _____

4. How many letters are in the English alphabet? _____

5. In what letter do all simple Latin verbs end? _____

B. Translate into English.

1. oro _____

2. amo _____

3. porto _____

4. Deus _____

5. luna _____

6. specto _____

7. gloria _____

8. ambulo _____

9. via _____

10. libero _____

C. Translate into Latin.

1. Hello (to one) _____

2. student _____

3. stand up (to many) _____

4. goodbye (to one) _____

5. teacher (female) _____

6. teacher (male) _____

D. Fill in the blanks.

_____. Sanctus, Sanctus _____ Dominus Deus

Sabbaoth. Pleni sunt Caeli et terra, _____Tua. Hosanna in excelsis.

Benedictus qui venit in nomine _____. Hosanna in excelsis. Amen.

Test II: Lessons 6-10

Nomen:_____

A. Answer the following questions in English.

1. What part of speech is a person, place, or thing? _____

2. What letter do many simple nouns end in? _____

3. What is an English word that comes from a Latin root word? _____

4. Name four months that have Latin numbers in them? _____

_____ , _____, _____

5. List two derivatives for femina. _____ , _____

B. Translate into English.

1. regina _____

2. unda _____

3. patria _____

4. herba _____

5. fortuna _____

6. aqua _____

7. cena _____

8. corona _____

9. silva _____

10. mensa _____

C. Write the Latin numbers 1-10.

1. _____   6. _____

2. _____   7. _____

3. _____   8. _____

4. _____   9. _____

5. _____   10. _____

D. Fill in the blanks.

Gloria _____, et _____ et Spiritui Sancto.

_____ erat in principio et _____ et

_____ et in saecula saeculorum. Amen.

A. Answer the following questions in English.

1. What do you call a specific person, place, or thing?_____

2. What part of speech shows relationship? _____

3. What part of speech describes a verb? _____

4. What part of speech describes a noun?_____

5. What part of speech replaces a noun? _____

B. Translate into English.

1. inter   _____   6. ex   _____

2. Italia   _____   7. longus   _____

3. contra   _____   8. clam   _____

4. altus   _____   9. semper   _____

5. novus   _____   10. nunc   _____

C. Translate into Latin.

1. I came, I saw, I conquered _____

2. nurturing mother _____

3. Mary   _____

4. much   _____

5. under   _____

6. Rome   _____

7. above   _____

8. wonder of the world _____

9. good   _____

10. never   _____

D. Fill in the Blanks.

_____ Domine nos et haec Tua _____ quae de Tua

largitate _____ sumpturi per _____ Dominum nostrum.

Amen.

Test IV: Lessons 16- 20

Nomen:_____

A. Answer the following questions in English.

1. What is the most common verb? _____

2. What tense describes things that will happen? _____

3. What are groups of pictures in the sky made of stars called? _____

4. What tense describes things that are happening? _____

5. The "to be" verb shows what? _____

B. Translate into English.

1. Pisces   _____   6. Gemini   _____

2. Cancer   _____   7. Taurus   _____

3. Leo   _____   8. Scorpio   _____

4. Libra   _____   9. Capricorn   _____

5. Aries   _____   10. Aquarius   _____

C. Translate into English.

1. sum   _____   4. sumus   _____

2. es   _____   5. estis   _____

3. est   _____   6. sunt   _____

1. possum   _____   4. possumus   _____

2. potes   _____   5. potestis   _____

3. potest   _____   6. possunt   _____

1. bo   _____   4. bimus   _____

2. bis   _____   5. bitis   _____

3. bit   _____   6. bunt   _____

D. Fill in the Blanks.

_____ noster, qui es in Caelis Sanctificetur _____ Tuum.

Adveniat _____ Tuum. Fiat voluntas Tua _____ in

Caelo et in _____ .

A. Answer the following questions in English.

1. What kind of word goes with a declension? _____

2. What kind of word goes with a conjugation? _____

3. What are two reasons you would conjugate a verb? _____

4. What goes at the end of question sentences? _____

B. Translate into English.

1. E pluribus unum   _____

2. Ego amo te   _____

3. sicut   _____

4. etiam   _____

5. non   _____

6. quis   _____

7. ubi   _____

8. optime   _____

9. finis   _____

10. cur   _____

C. Write the first conjugation.

_____   _____

_____   _____

_____   _____

D. Write the first declension singular and plural.

_____   _____

_____   _____

_____   _____

_____   _____

_____   _____

E. Fill in the blanks.

Panem _____ cotidianum da nobis hodie et dimmite nobis

_____ nostra _____ et nos dimittimus debitoribus nostris

et ne nos inducas in tentationem _____ libera nos a malo.

Test Answer Key

Test I

1. verbs
2. 5
3. w
4. 26
5. o

1. I pray
2. I love
3. I carry
4. God
5. moon
6. I look at
7. glory
8. I walk
9. road
10. I free

1. salve
2. discipulus
3. surgite
4. vale
5. magistra
6. magister

1. Oremus
2. Sanctus
3. gloria
4. Domini

Test II

1. noun
2. a
3. derivative
4. September, October, November, December
5. female, feminine

1. queen
2. wave
3. country
4. herb
5. luck
6. water
7. dinner
8. crown
9. forest
10. table

1. unus
2. duo
3. tres

4. quattor
5. quinque
6. sex
7. septem
8. octo
9. novem
10. decem

1. patri
2. filio
3. sicut
4. nunc
5. semper

Test III

1. Proper Noun
2. preposition
3. adverb
4. adjective
5. pronoun

1. between
2. Italy
3. against
4. high, deep
5. new
6. out of
7. long
8. secretly
9. always
10. now

1. veni, vidi, vici
2. alma mater
3. Maria
4. multus
5. sub
6. Roma
7. supra
8. stupor mundi
9. bonus
10. numquam

1. Benedic
2. dona
3. sumus
4. Christum

Test Answer Key

Test IV.

1. To be
2. future tense
3. constellations
4. present tense
5. existence

1. fish
2. crab
3. lion
4. scales
5. ram
6. twins
7. bull
8. scorpion
9. goat
10. water carrier

1. I am
2. you (s) are
3. he, she, it is
4. we are
5. you (pl) are
6. they are

1. I can
2. you (s) can
3. he, she, it can
4. we can
5. you (pl) can
6. they can

1. I will
2. you (s) will
3. he, she, it will
4. we will
5. you (pl) will
6. they will

1. Pater
2. nomen
3. regnum
4. sicut
5. terra

Test V.

1. noun
2. verb
3. who did the action, when they did the action
4. question mark, ?

1. one out of many
2. I love you
3. as
4. also
5. not
6. who
7. where
8. excellent
9. the end
10. why

Conjugations:

amo	amamus
amas	amatis
amat	amant

a	ae
ae	arum
ae	is
am	as
a	is

1. nostrum
2. debita
3. sicut
4. sed

Vocabulary Drill Form

CD EXERCISE FORM (reproducible)

LESSON _____

DATE ____ / ____ / ____

Listen to the CD and repeat the words, sayings, and forms after the teacher. Then write what you have practiced orally on this sheet in Latin and in English and record the date. Do this exercise at least three times for each lesson.

VOCABULARY

LATIN SAYINGS

1 _____

2 _____

3 _____

Grammar Drill Form

Prima Latina

2ND EDITION

PRONUNCIATION RULES

The Alphabet

The Latin alphabet has no "w". Words with "y" are of Greek origin.

Vowels

In Christian Latin vowels are usually long.

Vowel	Long	Example
a	'father' (ah)	ambulo
e	'they' (ay)	deus
i	'machine' (ee)	via
o	'no' (oh)	toga
u	'rule' (oo)	luna

Sometimes the vowels **e** and **i** tend toward the short vowel sounds ('Ed','it') as in 'mensa' and 'et'.

Diphthongs and digraphs

Digraph	Pronunciation	Example
ae	like *e* in 'they' (ay)	caelum
oe	like *e* in 'they' (ay)	proelium

Diphthong		
au	like ou in cow (ow)	laudo, nauta

Consonants

Most of the consonants are pronounced as in English, with the following exceptions.

Consonant	Pronunciation	Examples
c	soft before *e, i, ae, oe,* like *ch* in 'charity'	decem, caelum
c	hard before other letters, like *c* as in 'cut'	clamo, corona
g	soft before *e, i, ae, oe* like *g* as in 'germ'	regina, gemini
g	hard before other letters like *g* as in 'go'	toga, navigo
gn	like *gn* as in 'lasagne'	pugno
j	like *y* as in 'yet'	Jesus, judico
s	like *s* as in 'sing' (never like *z*)	tres, mensa
sc	like sh	discipulus
t	like *tsee*, when followed by *i* and a vowel	etiam

Prima Latina
Lessons

Practical Latin

Salve!   – Hello! (to one person)

Salvete!   – Hello! (to more than one person)

Lesson – The Alphabet

The building blocks of any language are the letters used to make words.

The English Alphabet

There are *26 letters* in the English alphabet.

The **alphabet** is made up of two types of letters:

     vowels   and   **consonants**.

A,E,I,O,U	**BCD FGH JKLMN PQRST VWXYZ** (all letters that are not vowels)

The Latin Alphabet

The Latin alphabet looks like the English alphabet EXCEPT:

There are only *25 letters* in the Latin **alphabet.**

The Latin alphabet has no **W**!

Latin has the same vowels as English, **A,E,I,O,U,** but they sound a little different. Here are the Latin Vowel sounds.

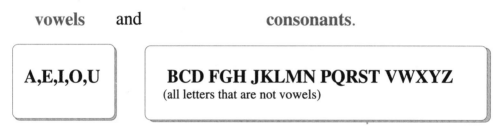

Vowel	Latin Sound
A	ah, as in father
E	ay, as in way
I	ee, as in see
O	oh, as in no
U	oo, as in boo

** Remember

Latin **E** sounds like an English long **A**.

Latin **I** sounds like an English long **E**.

Vocabulary

Practice saying the Latin **vowels** in each word.

1. ambulo		I walk
2. via		road
3. Deus		God
4. toga		toga
5. luna		moon

Latin Prayers

Oremus   **Let us pray**

Say this before each prayer.

Derivatives

ambulance	--a vehicle to carry those who cannot walk to the hospital (n.)
viaduct	--a roadway or bridge on piers (n.)
deity	--a god (n.)
lunar	--having to do with the moon (adj.)

Review Questions

1. How many letters are in the English alphabet? ___26___

2. How many letters are in the Latin alphabet? ___25___

3. What letter is missing from the Latin alphabet? ___W___

4. What are the two kinds of letters in the English alphabet? _____

   ___vowels & consonants___

Translation

1. toga   ___toga___

2. Deus   ___God___

3. ambulo   ___I walk___

4. luna   ___moon___

5. via   ___road___

Speaking Latin —Listen to the Lesson 1 track on your Prima Latina CD—

☐ Practice saying the Latin vowel sounds in order…ah, ay, ee, oh, oo.
Can you say them five times in a row?
How fast can you correctly say them?

☐ Practice saying, "Salve" or "Salvete" to your parents, brothers and sisters, or friends this week.

☐ Begin the prayer before each meal with "Oremus."

☐ Say each vocabulary word and its meaning five times.

Write and Learn

1. Write out the English alphabet.

   Circle the vowels and underline the consonants.

   (A) B C D (E) F G H (I) J K L M N (O) P Q R S T (U) V W X Y Z

   _____

2. Write out the Latin alphabet for practice. Make sure to leave out or cross out the **W**!

   A B C D E F G H I J K L M N O P Q R S T U V ✗ X Y Z

   _____

3. Write each vocabulary word and its meaning twice.

   1. _____ambulo_____   _____I walk_____
      _____ambulo_____   _____I walk_____

   2. _____via_____   _____road_____
      _____via_____   _____road_____

   3. _____Deus_____   _____God_____
      _____Deus_____   _____God_____

   4. _____toga_____   _____toga_____
      _____toga_____   _____toga_____

   5. _____luna_____   _____moon_____
      _____luna_____   _____moon_____

Fun Practice: Draw a line to match the letter with its Latin sound.

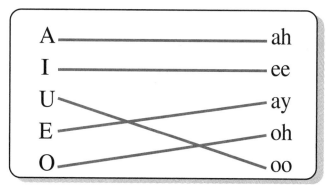

Practical Latin

Magister – Teacher (male)   Magistra – Teacher (female)

Lesson – Consonants and Diphthongs

Consonant Sounds:

Consonants	Latin Sound
c (before e, i, ae, & oe is soft)	ch, as in charity
c (before all other letters is hard)	k, as in cat
g (before e, i, ae, & oe is soft)	g, as in germ
g (before all other letters is hard)	g, as in good
j	y, as in yes
s	s, as in soap

Compare the soft and hard sounds of *c* and *g* in Latin & English:
- The soft *c* in Latin sounds like "ch" as in charity.
- The soft *c* in English sounds like "s" as in ceiling.
- The hard *c* is the same in Latin and English.
- The soft and hard *g* are the same in Latin and English.

Diphthongs:

In Latin, sometimes two letters have only one sound.
These letter pairs are called **diphthongs.**

Diphthongs	Latin Sound
ae	ay, as in way (English long A)
oe	ay, as in way (English long A)
au	ow, as in loud

Vocabulary

Practice saying the **consonant** sounds and **diphthongs**.

1. gloria	glory
2. Jesus	Jesus
3. laudo	I praise
4. clamo	I shout
5. caelum	heaven

Latin Prayers (The Sanctus)

* Each week, learn the bold portion of the prayer and add it to what you know.

Sanctus, Sanctus, Sanctus
Dominus Deus Sabbāoth.
Pleni sunt caeli et terra gloria Tua.
Hosanna in excelsis.
Benedictus qui venit in nomine Domini.
Hosanna in excelsis.

Holy, Holy, Holy
Lord God of Hosts.
Heaven and earth are full of Your glory.
Hosanna in the highest.
Blessed is he who comes in the name of the Lord.
Hosanna in the highest.

Derivatives

glorious	-- wonderful (adj.)
glorify	-- to exalt, worship or honor (v.)
Jesuit	-- a Roman Catholic order for men, called the Society of Jesus (n.)
laud	-- to praise (v.)
proclamation	-- an official announcement (n.)
celestial	-- heavenly (adj.)

Review Questions

1. How many letters are in the English alphabet? ___26___
2. What are the letters **A,E,I,O,U** called? ___Vowels___
3. What does a Latin **E** sound like? ___English long A (ay, as in way)___
4. What does a Latin **I** sound like? ___English long E (ee, as in see)___
5. What does a Latin **O** sound like? ___English O (oh, as in no)___

Lesson 2 Questions

1. How many letters are in the Latin alphabet? ___25___
2. What consonant is missing in the Latin alphabet? ___W___
3. What do you call two vowels that make one sound? ___dipthong___
4. What does a **J** sound like in Latin? ___Y___
5. List three diphthong pairs. ___ae, oe, au___

Translation

1. caelum ___heaven___
2. gloria ___glory___
3. Jesus ___Jesus___
4. laudo ___I praise___
5. clamo ___I shout___

Speaking Latin --Listen to the Lesson 2 track on your Prima Latina CD--

☐ Think of an English word that uses the following Latin consonant sounds:

hard g, as in gloria ___gate, ...___

soft g, as surgite ___ginger, ...___

soft c, as in caelum ___church, ...___

hard c, as in clamo ___camp, ...___

☐ Say each vocabulary word and its meaning five times.

☐ Address your teacher as "Magister" or "Magistra" from now on.

☐ Practice saying the Latin Prayers from Lessons 1 and 2, the Sanctus, five times.

Write and Learn

1. Write the six Latin consonants in the lesson and the Latin sounds that go with them.

c (soft before e, i, ae, & oe)	ch, as in charity
c (hard before other letters)	k, as in cat
g (soft before e, i, ae, & oe)	g, as in germ
g (hard before other letters)	g, as in good
j	y, as in yes
s	s, as in soap
~~t (before i)~~	~~tsee~~

2. Write the three diphthongs in the lesson and the Latin sounds that go with them.

ae - ay, as in way   oe - ay, as in way   au - ow, as in cow

3. Write each vocabulary word and its meaning twice.

1. _____   _____

   _____   _____

2. _____   _____

   _____   _____

3. _____   _____

   _____   _____

4. _____   _____

   _____   _____

5. _____   _____

   _____   _____

Fun Practice

Think of a poem or song to help you remember the vowel sounds.

Practical Latin

Surge – Stand up
(one person)

Surgite – Stand up
(more than one person)

Remember g before e and i is soft like g as in germ

Lesson – Verbs

Now that you have mastered letters and sounds, you can start making words! In any language, one of the most important kinds of words is a verb! Without verbs we wouldn't get anything done!

Verbs are *ACTION* words. In many cases you can see the action.

Examples of action words:

run   jump   kick   sing

An easy way to tell if a word is a **verb** is write or say it in the blank below.

Verb-Finder Sentence: Can I _____?

If the sentence makes sense, you probably have filled in the blank with a **verb.**

Examples:

Can I run?   ☑ YES, so **run** is a **verb.**

Can I jump?   ☑ YES, so **jump** is a **verb.**

Can I kick?   ☑ YES, so **kick** is a **verb.**

Can I table?   ☒ NO, I cannot table.
This doesn't make sense, so **table** is not a **verb.**

Vocabulary

Notice the **o** at the end of the Latin verbs below:

1. navig**o**	I sail
2. port**o**	I carry
3. or**o**	I pray
4. labor**o**	I work
5. spect**o**	I look at

Latin Prayers (The Sanctus)

Sanctus, Sanctus, Sanctus
Dominus Deus Sabbaoth.
Pleni sunt caeli et terra gloria Tua.
Hosanna in excelsis.
Benedictus qui venit in nomine Domini.
Hosanna in excelsis.

Holy, Holy, Holy
Lord God of Hosts.
Heaven and earth are full of Your glory.
Hosanna in the highest.
Blessed is he who comes in the name of the Lord.
Hosanna in the highest.

Derivatives

navigate	-- to steer a ship or plane (v.)
navy	-- a nation's ships OR a dark blue color (n.)
portable	-- something that can be carried (adj.)
airport	-- a place where aircraft land and take off (n.)
oral	-- spoken, or having to do with the mouth (adj.)
oratory	-- the art of public speaking (n.)
laboratory	-- a place for scientific work or research (n.)
labor	-- work, physical or mental exertion (n.)
spectacle	-- a remarkable sight (n.)
spectacular	-- remarkable, unusual (adj.)

Review Questions

1. List all the vowels in the English alphabet.   <u>A</u> , <u>E</u> , <u>I</u> , <u>O</u> , <u>U</u>

2. List the 3 diphthongs you learned about in Lesson 2. <u>au</u> , <u>ae</u> , <u>oe</u>

3. How many vowels make up one diphthong?   <u>two</u>

4. What does a **J** sound like in Latin?   <u>y</u>

5. How do you say, "Hello, teacher" (female) in Latin? <u>Salve, Magistra!</u>

Lesson 3 Questions

1. What are action words called? <u>verbs</u>

2. What is the helpful Verb-Finder sentence? <u>Can I   ?</u>

3. What do you notice about all the words in the vocabulary list? Hint: They are all verbs so they all end in the letter <u>O</u> .

4. How do you say, "Stand up" to one person in Latin? <u>Surge.</u>

Translation

1. oro   <u>I pray</u>

2. laboro   <u>I work</u>

3. porto   <u>I carry</u>

4. specto   <u>I look at</u>

5. navigo   <u>I sail</u>

Speaking Latin --Listen to the Lesson 3 track on your Prima Latina CD--

☐ Say each vocabulary word and its meaning five times. Practice using the vowel and consonant sounds you learned in Lessons 1 and 2.

(**Specto** has a short **e** sound, like "eh".)

☐ Every time you stand up today, practice saying, "Surge."

☐ Practice saying the Latin Prayer from Lessons 1, 2, 3, the Sanctus, five times.

Write and Learn

1. Write each vocabulary word and its meaning twice.

    1. _____   _____

        _____   _____

    2. _____   _____

        _____   _____

    3. _____   _____

        _____   _____

    4. _____   _____

        _____   _____

    5. _____   _____

        _____   _____

2. Think up 5 English verbs that are not in Lesson 3. Write them in the Verb-Finder Sentence below to make sure they are verbs. A sample has been done for you.

Verb Finder Sentence	**Yes?**
Can I _____Jump_____ ?	✓
1. Can I _____?	☐
2. Can I _____?	☐
3. Can I _____?	☐
4. Can I _____?	☐
5. Can I _____?	☐

Fun Practice   Circle the English verbs.

(walk)	tree	(snap)	(climb)
desk	book	(shout)	shoe
(wish)	(sit)	car	(look)
water	(sail)	beach	(laugh)

Practical Latin

Vale – Goodbye
(to one person)

Valete – Goodbye
(to more than one person)

Lesson – Invisible Verbs

Some verbs are **invisible verbs**.

You cannot always *see* them in *ACTION*, but they are verbs nonetheless.

Invisible action words are still verbs, they are just less obvious.

Examples of some **invisible verbs**:

think   hope   pray   love

Practice putting these **verbs** in our helpful **Verb-Finder sentence.**

> **Verb-Finder Sentence:** Can I _____?

Can I think?   ✓ YES! So **think** is a **verb.**

Can I hope?   ✓ YES! So **hope** is a **verb.**

Can I love?   ✓ YES! So **love** is a **verb.**

These words make sense in our Verb-Finder Sentence so they are verbs. Even though you can't always *see* someone think, hope, or love, it is something they can do.

Vocabulary

Notice the **o** at the end of the Latin verbs below.

1. amo	I love
2. adoro	I adore
3. habito	I live in
4. judico	I judge
5. paro	I prepare

Latin Prayers (The Sanctus)

Sanctus, Sanctus, Sanctus
Dominus Deus Sabbaoth.
Pleni sunt caeli et terra gloria Tua.
Hosanna in excelsis.
Benedictus qui venit in nomine Domini.
Hosanna in excelsis.

Holy, Holy, Holy
Lord God of Hosts.
Heaven and earth are full of Your glory.
Hosanna in the highest.
Blessed is he who comes in the name of the Lord.
Hosanna in the highest.

Derivatives

amorous	-- full of love (adj.)
adoration	-- great love or devotion (n.)
adorable	-- lovable (adj.)
habitat	-- a place where something or someone lives (n.)
judicial	-- having to do with judges, courts, and laws (adj.)
judgment	-- a decision or opinion (n.)
parachute	-- a device used to slow the speed of someone jumping from an airplane (n.)
preparation	-- getting ready, or making something in advance (n.)

Review Questions

1. What are action words called? _____ verbs _____

2. What do you call two vowels that make one sound? ____ dipthong ____

3. What letter is missing from the Latin alphabet? _____ W _____

4. What word means, "Let us pray" in Latin? _____ Oremus _____

5. What does a Latin **E** sound like? _____ ay, as in way (English long A) _____

Lesson 4 Questions

1. How can you tell if a word that does not show action is a verb (an invisible verb)?
   ____ Use the verb finder sentence: Can I _____ ? ____

2. What do you notice about all the Latin vocabulary words in Lesson 4?
   (Hint: look at the endings again.) ____ they all end in "O" ____

3. How do you say, "Goodbye" to one person in Latin? _____ Vale _____

4. How do you say, "Goodbye" to your entire family in Latin? ____ Valete ____

5. What do you call verbs you can't see in action? ____ invisible verbs ____

Translate

1. habito _____ I live in _____

2. amo _____ I love _____

3. paro _____ I prepare _____

4. judico _____ I judge _____

5. adoro _____ I adore _____

Speaking Latin --Listen to the Lesson 4 track on your Prima Latina CD--

☐ Say each vocabulary word and its meaning five times.

☐ Practice the vowel and consonant sounds you learned in Lessons 1 and 2. Say each five times.

☐ Say, "Goodbye" to your family in Latin this week.

☐ Practice Saying the Latin Prayers from Lessons 1 through 4, the Sanctus, five times.

Write and Learn

1. Write each vocabulary word and its meaning twice.

   1. _____   _____
      _____   _____

   2. _____   _____
      _____   _____

   3. _____   _____
      _____   _____

   4. _____   _____
      _____   _____

   5. _____   _____
      _____   _____

2. Think of eight invisible verbs in English. Write them on the lines below. Use the Verb-Finder sentence to make sure you are listing verbs.

   _____   _____   _____   _____

   _____   _____   _____   _____

Fun Practice

Get your favorite storybook. Find 6 invisible verbs while you read.

   _____   _____   _____

   _____   _____   _____

Practical Latin

Discipulus – student   Discipuli   – students
(sc has a 'sh' sound)

Lesson – Latin Verbs

ENGLISH VERBS

In English, verbs can start with any letter, end with any letter, and be as long or short as any other word.

English verbs look the same as any other English word.
Because you can't tell an English verb by looking at it, we have to use our Special Verb-Finder Sentence

LATIN VERBS

In Latin, **verbs** in their dictionary form look similar.

In a vocabulary list, Latin verbs all end in the letter "o"!

So, in English, we have to decide if a word is a verb by **thinking** about it.
But, in this book, we can usually decide if a Latin word is a verb by simply **looking** at it.

Vocabulary

Notice the o at the end of the Latin verbs below.

1. libero	I free
2. narro	I tell
3. pugno	I fight
4. supero	I conquer
5. voco	I call

Latin Prayers (The Sanctus)

Sanctus, Sanctus, Sanctus
Dominus Deus Sabbaoth.
Pleni sunt caeli et terra gloria Tua.
Hosanna in excelsis.

Holy, Holy, Holy
Lord God of Hosts.
Heaven and earth are full of Your glory.
Hosanna in the highest.

Benedictus qui venit in nomine Domini.
Hosanna in excelsis.

Blessed is he who comes in the name of the Lord.
Hosanna in the highest.

Derivatives

liberty	-- freedom (n.)
narrate	-- to tell about a story or event (v.)
narrator	-- the person telling about the story or event (n.)
pugnacious	-- in a fighting spirit (adj.)
superior	-- excellent (adj.)
vocal	-- something to do with speaking or singing (adj.)
vocabulary	-- a list of words (n.)

Review Questions

1. How would you describe a verb? _____ an action word _____

2. Name two types of letters in the alphabet. _____ vowels and consonants _____

3. List three Latin action verbs you have learned so far. _____ navigo, porto, oro _____
   _____ laboro, specto, libero, narro, pugno, supero, voco _____

4. List three Latin invisible verbs you have learned so far. _____ amo, adoro, _____
   _____ habito, judico, paro _____

5. How do you say, "Goodbye, Teacher" (male) in Latin? _____ Vale, Magister! _____

Lesson 5 Questions

1. In what letter do all simple Latin verbs end? _____ O _____

2. Is the letter at the end of all English verbs the same? _____ no _____

3. What is the Latin word for *one* student? _____ discipulus _____

4. What is the Latin word for *many* students? _____ discipuli _____

Translate

1. voco _____ I call _____

2. supero _____ I conquer _____

3. narro _____ I tell _____

4. pugno _____ I fight _____

5. libero _____ I free _____

Speaking Latin --Listen to the Lesson 5 track on your Prima Latina CD--

☐ Say each vocabulary word and its meaning five times. Practice the vowel and consonant sounds you learned in Lessons 1 and 2.

☐ Practice saying the Latin Prayers from Lessons 1 through 5, the Sanctus, five times.

Write and Learn

1. Write each vocabulary word and its meaning twice.

    1. _____   _____

        _____   _____

    2. _____   _____

        _____   _____

    3. _____   _____

        _____   _____

    4. _____   _____

        _____   _____

    5. _____   _____

        _____   _____

2. Think of eight verbs you performed today. Write them below, in the order you completed them. Put an **A** by the action verbs and an **I** by the invisible verbs.

    _____   _____

    _____   _____

    _____   _____

    _____   _____

Fun Practice

Circle the Latin verbs.

terra	(voco)	(paro)	Roma
(porto)	herba	aqua	(laboro)
via	(specto)	(navigo)	memoria
Italia	(laudo)	lingua	(voco)

Vocabulary

Verbs

laudo	I praise
clamo	I shout
ambulo	I walk
navigo	I sail
porto	I carry
oro	I pray
laboro	I work
specto	I look at
amo	I love
adoro	I adore
habito	I live in
judico	I judge
paro	I prepare
libero	I free
narro	I tell
pugno	I fight
supero	I conquer
voco	I call

Nouns

via	road
Deus	God
toga	toga
luna	moon
gloria	glory
Jesus	Jesus
caelum	heaven

> **Latin Song--** on *Lingua Angelica CD*
>
> "Dona Nobis Pacem"
>
> -Grant us Peace

Practical Latin

salve	hello (to one person)
salvete	hello (to more than one person)
magister	teacher (male)
magistra	teacher (female)
surge	stand up (to one person)
surgite	stand up (to more than one person)
vale	goodbye (to one person)
valete	goodbye (to more than one person)
discipulus	student
discipuli	students

Latin Prayers – The Sanctus

Sanctus, Sanctus, Sanctus	Holy, Holy, Holy
Dominus Deus Sabbaoth.	Lord God of Hosts.
Pleni sunt caeli et terra gloria Tua.	Heaven and earth are full of Your glory.
Hosanna in excelsis.	Hosanna in the highest.
Benedictus qui venit in nomine Domini.	Blessed is he who comes in the name of the Lord.
Hosanna in excelsis.	Hosanna in the highest.

EXERCISES for Review Lesson 1 (Lessons 1-5)

A. Copy all vocabulary words and translate.

Extra: Write one derivative next to each word.

	Word	Translation	Derivative
1.	_____	_____	_____
2.	_____	_____	_____
3.	_____	_____	_____
4.	_____	_____	_____
5.	_____	_____	_____
6.	_____	_____	_____
7.	_____	_____	_____
8.	_____	_____	_____
9.	_____	_____	_____
10.	_____	_____	_____
11.	_____	_____	_____
12.	_____	_____	_____
13.	_____	_____	_____
14.	_____	_____	_____
15.	_____	_____	_____
16.	_____	_____	_____
17.	_____	_____	_____
18.	_____	_____	_____
19.	_____	_____	_____
20.	_____	_____	_____
21.	_____	_____	_____
22.	_____	_____	_____
23.	_____	_____	_____
24.	_____	_____	_____
25.	_____	_____	_____

B. Answer the following questions in English.

1. How many letters are in the Latin alphabet? __25__
2. What letter is missing from the Latin alphabet? __W__
3. How many vowels are there? __5__
4. What does a **J** sound like in Latin? __Y, as in yes__
5. What does an **E** sound like in Latin? __English long A (ay, as in way)__
6. What does an **I** sound like in Latin? __English long E(ee, as in see)__
7. What are the two kinds of letters? __vowels & consonants__
8. What are words that show action called? __verbs__
9. In what letter do all simple Latin verbs end? __o__
10. What sentence helps you determine if a word is a verb? __Can I _____ ?__

C. Practice saying the Sanctus completely.

Say it five times from memory. Write it once in Latin for practice.

Oremus.

Sanctus, Sanctus, Sanctus

Dominus Deus Sabbaoth.

Pleni sunt caeli et terra gloria Tua.

Hosanna in excelsis.

Benedictus qui venit in nomine Domini.

Hosanna in excelsis.

D. Answer the following questions in Latin.

1. What do you say when you first see someone? __Salve!__

2. What would you call your female teacher? __magistra__

   What would you call your male teacher? __magister__

3. What does your teacher tell the class before the Pledge of Allegiance? __surgite__

4. What do you say when you are leaving your entire family? __valete__

   What do you say when you are leaving a friend? __vale__

5. What do you call yourself when you are in school? __discipulus__

E. Lingua Angelica Extra:
Sing, "Dona Nobis Pacem" with the CD.
Write the Latin words once and translate.

_____

_____

_____

_____

_____

_____

_____

Practical Latin

Deo Gratias   – Thanks be to God

Lesson – Nouns

Without nouns there would be no need for verbs. Who or what would do the ACTION? You are a **noun**. Your house, your dog, and your pencil are nouns, too.

> A **noun** is a *PERSON*, a *PLACE*, or a *THING.*
>
> Our **Noun-Finder** asks 3 questions:

> 1. Is it a PERSON?
> 2. Is it a PLACE?
> 3. Is it a THING?

If the answer is *yes* to just *one* of the questions, the word is a noun.

Example: girl

    Is it a **person**? ✓ Yes! A girl is a person, so **girl** is a **noun**.

Example: flower

    Is it a **person**? ☒ No, a flower is not a person.
    Is it a **place**? ☒ No, a flower is not a place.
    Is it a **thing**? ✓ Yes! A flower is a thing, so **flower** is a **noun**.

Example: jump

    Is it a **person**? ☒ No, a jump is not a person.
    Is it a **place**? ☒ No, a jump is not a place.
    Is it a **thing**? ☒ No, jump is not a thing, so **jump** is **NOT** a **noun**.

Vocabulary

Notice the **a** ending on each of these Latin nouns below.

1. regin**a**	queen
2. stell**a**	star
3. silv**a**	forest
4. terr**a**	earth
5. und**a**	wave
6. vit**a**	life

Latin Prayers (The Doxology)

Gloria Patri,
et Filio, et Spiritui Sancto.
Sicut erat in principio,
et nunc, et semper,
et in saecula saeculorum. Amen.

– Glory be to the Father,
– Son, and Holy Spirit.
– As it was in the beginning,
– is now, and ever shall be,
– world without end. Amen.

Derivatives

regal	-- like a king or queen, befitting royalty (adj.)
stellar	-- having to do with a star, outstanding (adj.)
constellation	-- a group of stars that form a picture (n.)
Pennsylvania	-- a state of the North East U.S. (proper noun)
territory	-- area of land (n.)
undulating	-- wave-like motion (n.)
vital	-- extremely important (adj.)
vitamin	-- a natural substance that is essential to health (n.)

EXERCISES for Lesson 6

Review Questions

1. Practice saying all the vowel sounds in Latin.

2. Practice saying the six Latin consonant sounds from Lesson 2.

3. How do you say, "Stand up" (to many) in Latin? _Surgite_

4. How do you say, "Let us pray" in Latin? _Oremus_

5. How do you say, "Hello, students" (many) in Latin? _Salvete, discipuli_

Lesson 6 Questions

1. A noun is a _person_ , _place_ , or _thing_ .

2. List five nouns you can see right now. _____ , _____ ,

_____ _____ _____

3. What are the three questions we use to see if a word is a noun?

1. _Is it a person?_

2. _Is it a place?_

3. _Is it a thing?_

4. In the Noun-Finder, how many questions have to be YES for a word to be a noun?
only one

5. What kind of noun are you: a person, place, or thing? _you are a person._

Translate

1. unda _wave_

2. terra _earth_

3. stella _star_

4. vita _life_

5. silva _forest_

6. regina _queen_

32

Speaking Latin --Listen to the Lesson 6 track on your Prima Latina CD--

☐ Say each vocabulary word and its meaning five times. Practice your pronunciation.

☐ Practice saying the Latin Prayer from Lesson 6, the Doxology, five times. Write it once with the English translation.

Gloria Patri,   – Glory be to the Father,

☐ Say, "Deo Gratias" when you are thankful this week.

Write and Learn

Write each vocabulary word and its meaning twice.

1. _____   _____

   _____   _____

2. _____   _____

   _____   _____

3. _____   _____

   _____   _____

4. _____   _____

   _____   _____

5. _____   _____

   _____   _____

6. _____   _____

   _____   _____

Fun Practice

Draw a picture of your neighborhood. Label all of the nouns.

Practical Latin

Mea Culpa   – my fault

Lesson – Latin Nouns

Like verbs, we can recognize **Latin nouns** in their dictionary forms by their endings. In Latin, there are five groups of nouns.
In the first group all of the nouns end in **A.**

English nouns are like English verbs; they can end in any letter. In the example below, notice that both of the Latin nouns end in **a**, but the endings for the English words are different.

Example:

Latin Noun	English Noun
aqu**a**	wate**r**
patri**a**	countr**y**

So again, in English, we have to decide if a word is a **noun** by *thinking* about it. But, in this book, we can decide if a **Latin** word is a **noun** by simply *looking* at it.

Vocabulary

Notice the **a** at the end of the Latin nouns below.

1. aqu**a**	water
2. cen**a**	dinner
3. coron**a**	crown
4. mens**a**	table
5. patri**a**	country, fatherland

Latin Prayers (The Doxology)

Gloria Patri,
et Filio, et Spiritui Sancto.
Sicut erat in principio,
et nunc, et semper,
et in saecula saeculorum. Amen.

– Glory be to the Father,
– Son, and Holy Spirit.
– As it was in the beginning,
– is now, and ever shall be,
– world without end. Amen.

Derivatives

aquarium	-- a tank for keeping water animals (n.)
aquatic	-- relating to, or being in water (adj.)
coronation	-- the crowning of a king/queen (n.)
patriot	-- someone who loves his/her country (n.)
patriotic	-- showing a love for one's country (adj.)

Review Questions

1. What consonant is missing from the Latin alphabet? _____W_____

2. In what letter do simple verbs end? _____O_____

3. What does a **J** sound like in Latin? _____Y_____

4. What do we call verbs that have action but do not show it? ___invisible verbs___

5. How many vowels are there in the alphabet? _____5_____

Lesson 7 Questions

1. Name three ways to identify a noun.

   It is a __person__ , __place__ , or __thing__ .

2. In what letter do many simple Latin nouns end? __a__

Translate

1. mensa ___table___

2. patria ___country, fatherland___

3. aqua ___water___

4. corona ___crown___

5. cena ___dinner___

Speaking Latin --Listen to the Lesson 7 track on your Prima Latina CD--

☐ Say each vocabulary word and its meaning five times. Practice your pronunciation.

☐ Practice saying the Latin Prayers from Lessons 6 and 7, the Doxology, five times.

☐ Say, "mea culpa" whenever you make a mistake this week.

Write and Learn

Write each vocabulary word and its meaning twice.

1. _____   _____

   _____   _____

2. _____   _____

   _____   _____

3. _____   _____

   _____   _____

4. _____   _____

   _____   _____

5. _____   _____

   _____   _____

Fun Practice

Write a list (in English) of six nouns you see in the room.

Check ✔ person, place, or thing for each noun.

Noun	person, place, or thing		
_____	☐ person	☐ place	☐ thing
_____	☐ person	☐ place	☐ thing
_____	☐ person	☐ place	☐ thing
_____	☐ person	☐ place	☐ thing
_____	☐ person	☐ place	☐ thing
_____	☐ person	☐ place	☐ thing

Practical Latin

amicus	– friend
amici	– friends

Lesson – Derivatives

Derivatives are English words that come from Latin root words.
A derivative looks like its Latin root word and has a similar or related meaning.
You have been learning derivatives since lesson one!

Following are some **derivatives** for the vocabulary words in this book.
Notice the similarities in the spelling and meaning between the Latin root word and their **derivatives**.

Latin Word	*English Derivative*	*Translation*
1. vita	<u>vita</u>min	life

a vitamin is a natural substance necessary for life

| 2. terra | <u>terr</u>itory | earth |

a territory is an area of land

| 3. navigo | <u>navig</u>ate | I sail |

to navigate is to steer a ship or plane

| 4. porto | <u>port</u>able | I carry |

portable is something able to be moved or carried

| 5. oro | <u>or</u>al | I pray |

oral is having to do with the mouth

| 6. laboro | <u>labo</u>ratory | I work |

a laboratory is a place where scientists work

| 7. specto | <u>spect</u>ator | I look at |

a spectator is someone who watches an event

Vocabulary

Consider the English **derivatives** of these words.

Latin Word	English Derivative	Translation
1. herba	herb	plant
2. injuria	injury	injury
3. femina	female, feminine	woman
4. nauta	nautical, navy	sailor
5. fortuna	fortune, fortunate	luck

Latin Prayers (The Doxology)

Gloria Patri,
et Filio, et Spiritui Sancto.
Sicut erat in principio,
et nunc, et semper,
et in saecula saeculorum. Amen.

– Glory be to the Father,
– Son, and Holy Spirit.
– As it was in the beginning,
– is now, and ever shall be,
– world without end. Amen.

EXERCISES for Lesson 8   50

Review Questions ━━━━━━━━━━━━━━━━━━━━━━━━━━━━━

1. What is an action word called? _____verb_____

2. Which of the two kinds of letters, vowel or consonant, is the letter **S**?

   _____consonant_____

3. What is a person, place, or thing? _____noun_____

4. How do you say, "my fault" in Latin? _____mea culpa_____

5. How do you say, "Thanks be to God" in Latin? _____Deo Gratias_____

Lesson 8 Questions ━━━━━━━━━━━━━━━━━━━━━━━━━━━━

1. What do you call an English word that has a similar meaning to, and spelling as,

   a Latin word? _____derivative_____

2. What is a derivative of **nauta**? _____navy, nautical, ..._____

3. What is a derivative of **herba**? _____herb,..._____

4. What is a derivative of **femina**? _____female, feminine, ..._____

5. What is a derivative of **fortuna**? _____fortune, fortunate, ..._____

6. What is a derivative of **injuria**? _____injury,..._____

Translate ━━━━━━━━━━━━━━━━━━━━━━━━━━━━━━━━━━━━

1. femina _____woman_____

2. fortuna _____luck_____

3. injuria _____injury_____

4. nauta _____sailor_____

5. herba _____plant_____

/2

Speaking Latin --Listen to the Lesson 8 track on your Prima Latina CD--

☐ Say each vocabulary word and its meaning five times. Practice your pronunciation.

☐ Tell your friends, "Hello" and, "Goodbye" in Latin all week. Use the Latin word for friend when you have the chance.

Write and Learn

Write each vocabulary word and its meaning twice. Write the derivatives next to the word each time.

30

	Word	Derivative	Translation
1.	_____	_____	_____
	_____	_____	_____
2.	_____	_____	_____
	_____	_____	_____
3.	_____	_____	_____
	_____	_____	_____
4.	_____	_____	_____
	_____	_____	_____
5.	_____	_____	_____
	_____	_____	_____

Fun Practice

Can you think of other derivatives for the Latin vocabulary words you have learned?

On a separate sheet of paper, list the derivatives with the corresponding Latin word.

extra credit
! point
for each
word

Practical Latin

Sedete   – Sit Down
                                           (to many)

Lesson – Numbers 1-5

This week we will learn the numbers one through five (1-5) in Latin.

Vocabulary

Numbers

1. unus	1 (one)
2. duo	2 (two)
3. tres	3 (three)
4. quattuor	4 (four)
5. quinque	5 (five)

Latin Prayers (The Doxology)

Gloria Patri,	– Glory be to the Father,
et Filio, et Spiritui Sancto.	– Son, and Holy Spirit.
Sicut erat in principio,	– As it was in the beginning,
et nunc, et semper,	**– is now, and ever shall be,**
et in saecula saeculorum. Amen.	– world without end. Amen.

Derivatives

unite	-- to join or make one (v.)
unicorn	-- a mythical creature with a one horn (n.)
dual	-- double (adj.)
tertiary	-- third (adj.)
trio	-- a group of three (n.)
quartet	-- a group of four (n.)
quarter	-- a fourth of something (n.)
quintuplets	-- five babies born at the same time from the same mother (n.)

Review Questions

Respond to the following questions in Latin.

1. How do you say, "Thanks be to God"? _____ Deo Gratias _____
2. What do you call a group of your playmates? _____ amici _____
3. How do you say, "Hello, students"? _____ Salvete, discipuli _____
4. What is the opposite of, "Stand Up"? _____ sedete _____

Translate

1. quinque _____ five _____
2. duo _____ two _____
3. tres _____ three _____
4. quattuor _____ four _____
5. unus _____ one _____

Speaking Latin --Listen to the Lesson 9 track on your Prima Latina CD--

☐ Count from 1 to 5, five times. Practice your pronunciation.

☐ Practice saying the Latin Prayers from Lessons 6 through 9, the Doxology, five times.

☐ Say, "Sedete" each time you sit down this week.

Write and Learn

Write the words for numbers 1-5 in Latin five times each.

1. _____ unus _____
2. _____ duo _____
3. _____ tres _____
4. _____ quattuor _____
5. _____ quinque _____

13

Fun Practice

Draw a picture to illustrate each noun below.

Write a Latin description by each picture.

Note

In English, we add an **s** to make a noun plural.

In Latin, we add an **ae** to make the nouns you've learned plural.

(as you progress in Latin, you will learn several endings to make nouns plural)

Example: 4 moons – quattuor lun**ae**

4 Queens

5 Earths

Practical Latin

Anno Domini, A.D.   – In the Year of our Lord

Lesson – Numbers 6-10

Notice how some Latin numbers resemble the names of the months of our calendar.

Vocabulary

sex	6 (six)
septem	7 (seven)
octo	8 (eight)
novem	9 (nine)
decem	10 (ten)

Latin Prayers (The Doxology)

Gloria Patri,	– Glory be to the Father,
et Filio, et Spiritui Sancto.	– Son, and Holy Spirit.
Sicut erat in principio,	– As it was in the beginning,
et nunc, et semper,	– is now, and ever shall be,
et in saecula saeculorum. Amen.	**– world without end. Amen.**

Derivatives

semester	-- historically a six-month term of school (15 to 18 weeks now) (n.)
September	-- the seventh month of the Roman calendar (n.)
October	-- the eighth month of the Roman calendar (n.)
octagon	-- an eight-sided figure (n.)
November	-- the ninth month of the Roman calendar (n.)
December	-- the tenth month of the Roman calendar (n.)
decimal	-- based on the number 10 (adj.)

109

Review Questions

5

Use the Latin numbers 1-10 to answer the following questions.

1. How old are you?_____

2. How many ears do you have?___duo_____

3. How many siblings do you have? _____ (use "nullus" for none)

4. How many toes do you have?___decem_____

5. How many ice cream scoops do you want? _____

Lesson 10 Questions

4

What Latin number corresponds with the following months?

1. November _____novem_____

2. October _____octo_____

3. September _____septem_____

4. December _____decem_____

Speaking Latin --Listen to the Lesson 10 track on your Prima Latina CD--

2

☐ Say the numbers 1 through 10 in Latin five times. Practice your pronunciation.

☐ Practice saying the entire Doxology five times.

Write and Learn

20

1. Write the numbers 1 through 5 in Latin three times. Write the number next to the word.

unus	one
duo	two
tres	three
quattuor	four
quinque	five

Write and Learn

30 1. Write the numbers 6 through 10 in Latin five times. Write the number next to the word.

    6.   sex   six

    7.   septem   seven

    8.   octo   eight

    9.   novem   nine

    10.   decem   ten

35 2. Write the entire Doxology one time.

    Gloria Patri,

    et Filio, et Spiritui Sancto.

    Sicut erat in principio,

    et nunc, et semper,

    et in saecula saeculorum. Amen.

5 3. Write down the birthdays of five special people. Write **A.D.** at the end of each to signify that the person was born after the birth of Christ.

    _____   _____

    _____   _____

    _____

Fun Practice

8 Look around your house and count how many of the following items you have.
Write the quantity in Latin.

1. televisions _____ 5. bicycles _____

2. brooms _____ 6. couches _____

3. bedrooms _____ 7. fishing poles _____

4. toothbrushes _____ 8. automobiles _____

Vocabulary

Nouns

regina	queen
stella	star
silva	forest
terra	earth
unda	wave
aqua	water
cena	dinner
corona	crown
mensa	table
patria	country
herba	plant
injuria	injury
femina	woman
nauta	sailor
fortuna	luck
vita	life

Numbers

unus	one
duo	two
tres	three
quattuor	four
quinque	five
sex	six
septem	seven
octo	eight
novem	nine
decem	ten

Latin Song-- "Christus Vincit"

Christus Vincit--Christ conquers

Christus Regnat--Christ reigns

Christus Imperat--Christ rules

Practical Latin

Deo gratias	Thanks be to God
mea culpa	my fault
amicus	friend
amici	friends
Sedete	Sit down (to many)
Anno Domini (A.D.)	In the year of our Lord

Latin Prayers – The Doxology

Gloria Patri,	Glory be to the Father,
et Filio, et Spiritui Sancto.	Son, and Holy Spirit.
Sicut erat in principio,	As it was in the beginning,
et nunc, et semper,	is now, and ever shall be,
et in saecula saeculorum. Amen.	world without end. Amen.

A. Copy all vocabulary words and translate.

Extra: Write one derivative next to each word.

	Word	Translation	Derivative
1.	_____	_____	_____
2.	_____	_____	_____
3.	_____	_____	_____
4.	_____	_____	_____
5.	_____	_____	_____
6.	_____	_____	_____
7.	_____	_____	_____
8.	_____	_____	_____
9.	_____	_____	_____
10.	_____	_____	_____
11.	_____	_____	_____
12.	_____	_____	_____
13.	_____	_____	_____
14.	_____	_____	_____
15.	_____	_____	_____
16.	_____	_____	_____
17.	_____	_____	_____
18.	_____	_____	_____
19.	_____	_____	_____
20.	_____	_____	_____
21.	_____	_____	_____
22.	_____	_____	_____
23.	_____	_____	_____
24.	_____	_____	_____
25.	_____	_____	_____
26.	_____	_____	_____

B. Answer the following questions.

1. What part of speech is a person, place, or thing? noun
2. In what letter do nouns you have learned end? a
3. Name four months that are derivatives of Latin numbers. November

   December, October, September

C. Practice saying the Doxology completely.

Say it five times from memory. Write it once.

Gloria Patri,

et Filio, et Spiritui Sancto.

Sicut erat in principio,

et nunc, et semper,

et in saecula saeculorum. Amen.

D. Answer the following questions in Latin.

1. How could you end a prayer? Deo Gratias
2. What do you call people you like? amici
3. What do you do when you say the Pledge of Allegiance? surgite
4. What do you say when you make a mistake and take responsibility for it?

   mea culpa
5. What is the complete way to write what year this is?

   Anno Domini (A.D.)

   (Hint: is it before or after the birth of Christ?)

E. Lingua Angelica Extra: Sing, "Christus Vincit" with the CD.

Write the Latin words once and translate.

Notes

Practical Latin

Veni, vidi, vici   — I came, I saw, I conquered.
(Julius Caesar)

Lesson – Proper Nouns

A **proper noun** is a noun that names a *specific* person, place, or thing.

(Nouns that are not **proper nouns** are called "common nouns." The nouns we have learned about so far are common nouns.)

Example: **girl**
The noun **girl** can refer to any girl. **Girl** is a **common noun**.

The noun **Sylvia** refers only to the girl named Sylvia.
Sylvia is a **proper noun**.

An easy way to recognize a proper noun is by a **CAPITAL LETTER** for the first letter of the word.

Note: a common noun may have a capital first letter if it is at the beginning of a sentence, but, if it doesn't refer to a specific person, place, or thing, it is still a common noun.

Let's think of some other noun/proper noun pairs.

Common Noun	Proper Noun
country	Italy
state	Tennessee
girl	Sarah Hughes
boy	Julius Caesar
book	*Prima Latina*
game	Monopoly

Vocabulary

Notice the capital letters.

1.	Roma	Rome
2.	Italia	Italy
3.	Maria	Mary
4.	Marcus	Marcus
5.	Hispania	Spain

Latin Prayers (The Table Blessing)

Benedic, Domine, nos
et haec Tua dona
quae de Tua largitate
sumus sumpturi.
Per Christum Dominum nostrum. Amen.

-- Bless us, O Lord,
-- and these Your gifts
-- which from Your bounty
-- we are about to receive.
-- through Christ our Lord. Amen.

Derivatives

Roman — having to do with Rome (adj.)
Italian — having to do with Italy (adj.)
Spanish — having to do with Spain (adj.)
Hispanic — a Latin-American person who lives in the U.S. (n.)

Review Questions

What kind of word is each of the following: noun, verb, or proper noun?

1. bird   __noun__
2. jump   __verb__
3. Rome   __proper noun__
4. love   __verb__
5. Mary   __proper noun__

Lesson 11 Questions

1. A noun that names a specific person, place, or thing is called a __proper__ noun.

2. List three Latin proper nouns you know. _____,_____,_____

3. What is an easy way to recognize a proper noun? __It begins with a capital letter.__

4. Write a proper noun for each of the following nouns.

   boy   _____

   restaurant _____

   book   _____

   city   _____

Translate

1. Roma   __Rome__
2. Maria   __Mary__
3. Hispania   __Spain__
4. Marcus   __Mark__
5. Italia   __Italy__

Speaking Latin   --Listen to the Lesson 11 track on your Prima Latina CD--

☐ Say each vocabulary word and its meaning five times. Practice your pronunciation.

☐ Practice saying the Practical Latin saying, "Veni, vidi, vici" each time you accomplish something difficult.

☐ Practice saying the Latin Prayer from Lesson 11, the Table Blessing, before your mealtime prayer.

Write and Learn

1. Write each vocabulary word and its meaning twice.

   1. _____   _____

      _____   _____

   2. _____   _____

      _____   _____

   3. _____   _____

      _____   _____

   4. _____   _____

      _____   _____

   5. _____   _____

      _____   _____

Fun Practice

Write a list of ten common nouns. Match each with an appropriate proper noun.

	Common Noun	**Proper Noun**
Example	city	Atlanta
1.	_____	_____
2.	_____	_____
3.	_____	_____
4.	_____	_____
5.	_____	_____
6.	_____	_____
7.	_____	_____
8.	_____	_____
9.	_____	_____
10.	_____	_____

Practical Latin

Quo vadis?   – Where are you going?

Lesson – Prepositions

Prepositions are words that show a RELATIONSHIP between two words.
It helps to first think of **prepositions** as words that show the location or *position* of something. This is easy to remember because the word **position** is in the word pre**position**.

Examples of **prepositions** are:

under	on
in	above
out of	between
with	by

For example, think of a noun–let's say, "desk".
Now, let's think of *where the desk is...*

Is the desk *under* the roof?
Is it *on* the floor?
Is it flying *in* the air?
Is it *by* the wall?

The benefit of **prepositions** is that they help us know *where the desk is located.*

Vocabulary

These are Latin **prepositions.**

1. inter	between
2. sub	under
3. supra	above
4. ex	out of
5. contra	against

Latin Prayers (The Table Blessing)

Benedic, Domine, nos	-- Bless us, O Lord,
et haec Tua dona	**-- and these Your gifts**
quae de Tua largitate	-- which from Your bounty
sumus sumpturi.	-- we are about to receive.
Per Christum Dominum nostrum. Amen.	-- Through Christ our Lord. Amen.

Derivatives

interrupt	-- to make a break in conversation or action (v.)
intermediate	-- in the middle (adj.)
submarine	-- underwater ship (n.)
subway	-- underground railway (n.)
superb	-- above average, excellent (adj.)
exit	-- a way out (n.)
extraordinary	-- out of the ordinary, very unusual (adj.)
contrary	-- opposite or different (adj.)
contrast	-- to compare unlike things (v.)

Review Questions

Answer the following questions in English.

1. What is a word that shows action called? _____ verb _____

2. Who said, "Veni, vidi, vici"? _____ Julius Caesar _____

3. What is a specific person, place, or thing? _____ proper noun _____

4. What is an English word with a similar spelling and meaning to a Latin word?

_____ derivative _____

Lesson 12 Exercises

Use an English preposition in the vocabulary list to write a sentence describing the location of the following nouns. You decide where each item is located.

Example: The girl is *in* the house.

1. table _____

2. moon _____

3. toga _____

4. queen _____

5. boy _____

Translate

1. supra _____ above _____

2. contra _____ against _____

3. inter _____ between _____

4. sub _____ under _____

5. ex _____ out of _____

Speaking Latin   --Listen to the Lesson 12 track on your Prima Latina CD--

☐ Say each vocabulary word and its meaning five times. Practice your pronunciation.

☐ Say the Latin Prayers from Lessons 11 and 12, the Table Blessing, before your mealtime prayer.

☐ When you change locations this week, use Latin prepositions to identify where you are.

Write and Learn

1. Write each vocabulary word and its meaning three times.

Word	Meaning
1. _____	_____
_____	_____
2. _____	_____
_____	_____
3. _____	_____
_____	_____
4. _____	_____
_____	_____
5. _____	_____
_____	_____

Fun Practice

Draw a picture of a school scene on another sheet of paper. Describe the nouns in your picture using prepositions. Example: The floor is under the desk.

_____

_____

_____

_____

_____

Practical Latin

alma mater   – nurturing mother

Lesson – Pronouns

A **pronoun** is a word that *replaces* a noun or **pronoun**.

It *refers* to a person, place, or thing without actually saying a name.

English **pronouns** include:

I	we
you (s.)	you (pl.)
he	they
she	
it	

Example: Let's talk about Mary and her dog.

> We could say, **Mary** is pretty. **Mary** is 8 years old.
> **Mary** has a dog. **Mary's dog** has red hair.

But it is easier to take a break from using her name and use **pronouns**.

> Mary is pretty. **She** is 8 years old. **She** has a dog.
> **It** has red hair.

Pronoun letters are at the end of **verbs** in Latin.

You will learn later that using pronoun letters is the first step in *conjugating* verbs.

Singular (s.) and Plural (pl.)

Notice that *"you"* is listed twice in the English pronouns, once as singular (s.) and once as plural (pl.). *"You"* is tricky because it can be singular or plural. The pronoun *"you"* is singular or plural based on who is being addressed.

Singular *"you"* is addressed to one person. If Mary's mom tells her:

"*You* have homework to do." She is addressing a single person, Mary.

Plural *"you"* is addressed to more than one person. If Mary's teacher tells her class:

"*You* have homework to do." She is talking to a group of people, the class.

Grammar

These are **verb endings** (**pronoun letters**) in Latin. They go on the end of verbs and tell us which pronoun goes with a Latin verb. You will learn how to use these in the chapter on conjugating verbs. For now, just memorize the pronoun letters.

1. **o**	I
2. **s**	you
3. **t**	he, she, it
4. **mus**	we
5. **tis**	you (plural)
6. **nt**	they

Latin Prayers (The Table Blessing)

Benedic, Domine, nos
et haec Tua dona
quae de Tua largitate
sumus sumpturi.
Per Christum Dominum nostrum. Amen.

-- Bless us, O Lord,
-- and these Your gifts
-- which from Your bounty
-- we are about to receive.
-- Through Christ our Lord. Amen.

Review Questions

Answer the following questions in English.

1. What is an action word called? _____ verb _____

2. What is a specific noun called? _____ proper noun _____

3. What kind of word shows relationship? _____ preposition _____

4. What is a word that replaces a noun? _____ pronoun _____

5. What letter is missing from the Latin alphabet? _____ W _____

Lesson 13 Questions

Write the pronoun that would best replace the underlined words in the following sentences.

1. The boy climbed a tree. _____ he _____

2. The girls ran across the field. _____ they _____

3. My family goes to church. _____ ~~they~~ We _____

4. My desk is in the classroom. _____ it _____

5. Suzie drives a car. _____ she _____

Translate

What Latin verb endings (pronoun letters) correspond to the following pronouns?

1. you (singular) _____ s _____

2. I _____ o _____

3. we _____ mus _____

4. he, she, it _____ t _____

5. they _____ nt _____

6. you (plural) _____ tis _____

Speaking Latin --Listen to the Lesson 13 track on your Prima Latina CD--

☐ Say each verb ending and its corresponding pronoun five times.

Write and Learn

Write each verb ending and its corresponding pronoun twice.

1. _____   _____
   _____   _____

2. _____   _____
   _____   _____

3. _____   _____
   _____   _____

4. _____   _____
   _____   _____

5. _____   _____
   _____   _____

6. _____   _____
   _____   _____

Fun Practice

Write a song or poem to help you remember the verb endings.

_____

_____

_____

_____

_____

_____

_____

Practical Latin

Stupor Mundi   – wonder of the world

Lesson – Adjectives

Adjectives are words used to *modify* (or change) nouns or pronouns.
Adjectives *DESCRIBE* a person, place or thing.
They can be colors, sizes, numbers, or shapes, for example.

Adjectives modify nouns and pronouns and make them more interesting.
For example, think of a city. What kind of a city is it?
The words you use to describe it are **adjectives**.

Below, the adjectives are in bold print.

Is it **hot**?

Is it **big**?

Is it **old**?

Is it **crowded**?

Now, think of your room. Think of some **adjectives** to describe it.

What color is it?

What shape is it?

How big is it?

Vocabulary

Here are some Latin adjectives.

1. altus		high, deep
2. multus		much, many
3. bonus		good
4. longus		long
5. novus		new

Latin Prayers (The Table Blessing)

Benedic, Domine, nos
et haec Tua dona
quae de Tua largitate
sumus sumpturi.
Per Christum Dominum nostrum. Amen.

-- Bless us, O Lord,
-- and these Your gifts
-- which from Your bounty
-- we are about to receive.
-- Through Christ our Lord. Amen.

Derivatives

altitude	-- height (n.)
multiply	-- to increase (v.)
bonus	-- something extra (n.)
longitude	-- imaginary lines that run vertically on a globe (n.)
innovation	-- a new invention (n.)
novice	-- beginner (n.)
novel	-- new and unusual (adj.)

Review Questions ────────────────────

1. Practice saying the Sanctus from memory.
2. Write the Sanctus in full and translate.

Sanctus, Sanctus, Sanctus	Holy, Holy, Holy
Dominus Deus Sabbaoth.	Lord God of Hosts.
Pleni sunt caeli et terra, gloria Tua.	Heaven and earth are full of Your glory.
Hosanna in excelsis.	Hosanna in the highest.
Benedictus qui venit in nomine Domini.	Blessed is he who comes in the name of the Lord.
Hosanna in excelsis.	Hosanna in the highest.

Lesson 14 Questions ────────────────────

Answer the following questions in English.

1. What is another word for "modify"? _____ change or describe _____
2. What do adjectives do? _____ describe a person, place, or thing
3. What two kinds of words do adjectives modify? _____ nouns & pronouns _____
4. List three adjectives that describe you. _____, _____, _____ .
5. List three adjectives that describe your house. _____ ,

_____   _____

Translate ────────────────────

1. longus _____ long _____
2. bonus _____ good _____
3. novus _____ new _____
4. altus _____ high, deep _____
5. multus _____ much, many _____

Speaking Latin --Listen to the Lesson 14 track on your Prima Latina Cd--

☐ Say the vocabulary words five times. Practice your pronunciation.

☐ Practice saying "Wonder of the World" in Latin.

Write and Learn

Write each vocabulary word and its meaning twice.

1. _____   _____

   _____   _____

2. _____   _____

   _____   _____

3. _____   _____

   _____   _____

4. _____   _____

   _____   _____

5. _____   _____

   _____   _____

Fun Practice

Circle the words that may be adjectives.

(blue)	run	jump	in	tree
(two)	(square)	book	(new)	(high)
car	(good)	(long)	boy	Mary

Practical Latin

Nunc aut numquam   – Now or never

Lesson – Adverbs

Adverbs are words that modify (or change) **VERBS**. This is easy to remember because the word **VERB** is in the word AD**VERB.**

Adverbs describe **how**, **where**, **when**, or **why** a verb happens.
Many English **adverbs** can be identified by the letters **ly** at the end.

For example, let's choose a verb: walk.
>   Now, let's think of the different ways you can walk.
>   You may want to practice these.

>   You can:

walk quick*ly*	walk slow*ly*
walk loud*ly*	walk quiet*ly*
walk proud*ly*	walk sad*ly*

All the words above are **adverbs**. See how they modify or change the verb *walk*?

Adverbs can also tell *when* a verb happens.

>   Examples of this kind of **adverb** are:

now	never
often	always

Now, let's think of how these adverbs can modify walk
You can:

walk *now*	*never* walk
walk *often*	*always* walk

Vocabulary

Here are some Latin **adverbs**.

1.	clam	secretly
2.	numquam	never
3.	nunc	now
4.	saepe	often
5.	semper	always

Latin Prayers (The Table Blessing)

Benedic, Domine, nos	-- Bless us, O Lord,
et haec Tua dona	-- and these Your gifts
quae de Tua largitate	-- which from Your bounty
sumus sumpturi.	-- we are about to receive.
Per Christum Dominum nostrum. Amen.	**-- Through Christ our Lord. Amen.**

Review Questions

Answer the following questions in Latin.

1. What is Julius Caesar's most famous quote? _____ Veni, vidi, vici _____

2. How do you say, "Where are you going?" _____ Quo vadis? _____

3. How do you say, "nurturing mother" in Latin? ___ alma mater _____

4. What is the opposite of "Surgite"? _____ sedete _____

Lesson 15 Questions

1. What kinds of words do adverbs change or modify? _____ verbs _____

2. What is an easy way to remember what kind of word adverbs change? _____
   _____ the word verb is in adVERB _____

3. Name four things an adverb tells you. _ how, where, when, why _____

4. What is an easy way to recognize some English adverbs? _____
   _____ they sometimes have an "ly" at the end

Translate

1. saepe _____ often _____
2. semper _____ always _____
3. nunc _____ now _____
4. clam _____ secretly _____
5. numquam _____ never _____

Speaking Latin --Listen to the Lesson 15 track on your Prima Latina CD--

☐ Say each vocabulary word and its meaning five times. Practice your pronunciation.

☐ Say the Table Blessing in full before your meals this week.

☐ Practice saying "Now or Never" in Latin when there is something you need to finish.

Write and Learn

1. Write each vocabulary word and its meaning twice.

1. _____   _____

   _____   _____

2. _____   _____

   _____   _____

3. _____   _____

   _____   _____

4. _____   _____

   _____   _____

5. _____   _____

   _____   _____

2. Write the Table Blessing once in Latin. Recite it from memory in English

   Benedic, Domine, nos

   et haec Tua dona

   quae de Tua largitate

   sumus sumpturi.

   Per Christum Dominum nostrum. Amen.

Fun Practice

Decide if the words below are adjectives or adverbs. Check ✓ either "adjective" or "adverb" next to each word.

soon   ☐ adjective ✓ adverb   always   ☐ adjective ✓ adverb

quietly   ☐ adjective ✓ adverb   cold   ✓ adjective ☐ adverb

purple   ✓ adjective ☐ adverb   quickly ☐ adjective ✓ adverb

big   ✓ adjective ☐ adverb   small   ✓ adjective ☐ adverb

slowly   ☐ adjective ✓ adverb   often   ☐ adjective ✓ adverb

Vocabulary and Grammar

Proper Nouns

Roma	Rome
Italia	Italy
Maria	Mary
Marcus	Mark
Hispania	Spain

Prepositions

inter	between
sub	under
supra	above
ex	out of
contra	against

Adjectives

altus	high, deep
bonus	good
multus	much
longus	long
novus	new

Pronouns/Verb Endings

o	I
s	you
t	he, she, it
mus	we
tis	you (plural)
nt	they

Adverbs

clam	secretly
numquam	never
nunc	now
saepe	often
semper	always

> **Latin Song**--Refrain of "Adeste Fideles"
> Venite adoremus--O come let us adore Him,
> Venite adoremus--O come let us adore Him,
> Venite adoremus--O come let us adore Him,
> Dominum--Christ the Lord.

Practical Latin

Veni, vidi, vici	I came, I saw, I conquered.
Quo vadis?	Where are you going?
alma mater	nurturing mother
stupor mundi	wonder of the world
nunc aut numquam	now or never

Latin Prayers - The Table Blessing

Benedic, Domine, nos	Bless us, O Lord,
et haec Tua dona	and these Your gifts
quae de Tua largitate	which from Your bounty
sumus sumpturi.	we are about to receive.
Per Christum Dominum nostrum. Amen.	Through Christ our Lord. Amen.

A. Copy all vocabulary words and translate.

Extra: Write one derivative next to each word.

Word	**Translation**	**Derivative**
1. _____	_____	_____
2. _____	_____	_____
3. _____	_____	_____
4. _____	_____	_____
5. _____	_____	_____
6. _____	_____	_____
7. _____	_____	_____
8. _____	_____	_____
9. _____	_____	_____
10. _____	_____	_____
11. _____	_____	_____
12. _____	_____	_____
13. _____	_____	_____
14. _____	_____	_____
15. _____	_____	_____
16. _____	_____	_____
17. _____	_____	_____
18. _____	_____	_____
19. _____	_____	_____
20. _____	_____	_____
21. _____	_____	_____
22. _____	_____	_____
23. _____	_____	_____
24. _____	_____	_____
25. _____	_____	_____
26. _____	_____	_____

B. *Answer the following questions.*

1. What is a word that names a specific person, place or thing? ___proper noun___

2. What part of speech shows relationship and location? _____preposition_____

3. What part of speech describes a noun or pronoun? _____adjective_____

4. What part of speech describes a verb? _____adverb_____

C. *Practice saying the Table Blessing completely.*
Say it three times in Latin and three times in English from memory.

Benedic, Domine, nos	– Bless us, O Lord,
et haec Tua dona	– and these your gifts
quae de Tua largitate	– which from your bounty
sumus sumpturi.	– we are about to receive.
Per Christum Dominum nostrum. Amen.	– Through Christ our Lord. Amen

D. *Fill in blanks in Latin.* -- *be sure to review your Latin Sayings --*

1. What can you say when you accomplish something hard? _____Veni, vidi, vici._____

2. What is the Latin saying for, "nurturing mother"? _____alma mater_____

3. What can you say when you must get something finished? _nunc aut numquam_

4. What can you call something beautiful, like a rainbow? _____stupor mundi_____

5. How do you ask where someone is going? _____Quo vadis?_____

E. *Lingua Angelica Extra: Sing the Refrain of "Adeste Fideles" with the CD. Write the Latin words once and translate.*

_____

_____

_____

_____

_____

_____

Practical Latin

Semper Fidelis   – Always Faithful
                                 (Marine Corps motto)

Lesson – Constellations

Constellations are groups of stars that form pictures in the sky. They often have fantastic myths created by the very early Greek and Roman civilizations to explain them. Scientists and sailors use constellations to map the sky.

Pictures of the Constellations

Aquarius - water carrier
Aquarius, or Ganymede, was
the cupbearer to the gods

Aries - ram
This ram may have been the
one whose golden fleece
was the object of Jason's
quest

Cancer - crab
In his second labor, Hercules
was attacked by this giant
crab sent by Hera

Capricorn - goat
Pan changed himself into a
goat with a fish's tail

Gemini - twins
Zeus placed the Gemini twins,
Castor and Pollux, together in
the sky so they would never be
separated again

Virgo - maiden, virgin
The goddess of justice who
believed in people

Vocabulary

Here are the names of some constellations.

1. Aquarius   water carrier

2. Aries   ram

3. Cancer   crab

4. Capricorn   goat

5. Gemini   twins

6. Virgo   maiden, virgin

Latin Prayers (The Our Father or Lord's Prayer)

Pater Noster qui es in Caelis   – Our Father who is in Heaven

Review Questions _____

Answer the following questions in English.

1. What do you call words that modify verbs? _____ adverbs _____

2. In what letter do simple Latin verbs end? _____ O _____

3. In what letter do nouns in our first group end? _____ A _____

4. What do you call a word that shows a relationship or location? _preposition_

5. What do you call a word that describes a noun? _____ adjective _____

Lesson 16 Questions _____

1. What is a constellation? _____ a group of stars that form a picture _____

2. Who named them and told stories to explain them? _early Greeks and Romans_

3. Where can you see a constellation? _in the sky_

Translate _____

	Latin	English
	Virgo	maiden, virgin
	Aries	ram
	Cancer	crab
	Gemini	twins
	Aquarius	water carrier
	Capricorn	goat

Speaking Latin --Listen to the Lesson 16 track on your Prima Latina Cd--

☐ Say each vocabulary word and its meaning five times. Practice your pronunciation.

☐ Look for bumper stickers with "Semper Fidelis" or "Semper Fi" on them this week. Say the Marine Corps motto when when you see it.

Write and Learn

Write each vocabulary word and its meaning twice.

1. _____   _____

   _____   _____

2. _____   _____

   _____   _____

3. _____   _____

   _____   _____

4. _____   _____

   _____   _____

5. _____   _____

   _____   _____

6. _____   _____

   _____   _____

Fun Practice

Look in a science book to see pictures of the constellations. Draw and label the pictures you find.

Practical Latin

Repetite   – Repeat
                                (to many)

Lesson – More Constellations

Note the short mythical stories beneath each constellation. A myth is a traditional, ancient tale about supernatural beings or heros.

Pictures of the Constellations

Leo - lion
The lion Hercules fought for
three days and three nights

Libra - scales of justics
Scales used to weigh
good and evil

Pisces - fish
Aphrodite and Eros changed
themselves into fish to
escape a monster

Sagittarius - archer
The brave and wise centaur
Chiron, who tutored Achilles,
Hercules, and Asclepius

Scorpio - scorpion
Scorpio tried to kill the hunter
Orion

Taurus - bull
Zeus changed himself into a
bull to woo Europa

Vocabulary

Here are names of more constellations.

1. Leo	lion
2. Libra	scales of justice
3. Pisces	fish
4. Sagittarius	archer
5. Scorpio	scorpion
6. Taurus	bull

Latin Prayers (The Our Father or Lord's Prayer)

Sanctificetur nomen Tuum — Hallowed be Your name

Review Questions

1. Practice saying the Table Blessing.

2. Write the Table Blessing in full and translate.

Benedic, Domine, nos	Bless us, O Lord,
et haec Tua dona	and these Your gifts
quae de Tua largitate	which from Your bounty
sumus sumpturi.	we are about to receive.
Per Christum Dominum nostrum. Amen.	Through Christ our Lord. Amen.

Translate

Latin	English
Leo	lion
Scorpio	scorpion
Pisces	fish
Sagittarius	archer
Libra	scales of justice
Taurus	bull

Speaking Latin --Listen to the Lesson 17 track on your Prima Latina CD--

☐ Say each vocabulary word and its meaning five times. Practice your pronunciation.

☐ Politely say, "Repeat" in Latin this week when you need someone to repeat what they have said.

Write and Learn

Write each vocabulary word and its meaning twice.

1. _____ _____
   _____ _____

2. _____ _____
   _____ _____

3. _____ _____
   _____ _____

4. _____ _____
   _____ _____

5. _____ _____
   _____ _____

6. _____ _____
   _____ _____

Fun Practice

Look in a science book to see pictures of this week's constellations. On a separate piece of paper, draw and label the pictures you find.

Practical Latin

Quid agis?   – How are you?

Lesson – To Be Verb

The verb *to be* is the most common verb in any language. The *to be* verb shows existence, not action. This verb explains how we are, not how we act.

For example:
> I **am** a girl.
>
> You **are** tall.
>
> She **is** pretty.
>
> He **is** short.
>
> We **are** a family.
>
> They **are** happy.

Notice there are no other verbs in these sentences.

The words *is, am, are* take the place of an action or invisible verb.

Below are all the English forms of the *to be* verb in the present tense.

Singular		*Plural*	
I	am	we	are
you (s.)	are	you (pl.)	are
he, she, it	is	they	are

In Latin, the *to be* verb is irregular. If you look carefully at the *to be* verb, you will notice later that the endings resemble Latin verb endings.

86

Vocabulary

Notice the highlighted endings.

1.	sum	I am
2.	e**s**	you (s.) are
3.	e**st**	he, she, it is
4.	su**mus**	we are
5.	es**tis**	you (pl.) are
6.	su**nt**	they are

Latin Prayers (The Our Father or Lord's Prayer)

Adveniat regnum Tuum   – May Your kingdom come

Review Questions

Answer the following questions in Latin.

1. What do you call your friends? _____ amici _____

2. What does "A.D." mean? _____ Anno Domini _____

3. What is the Marine Corps motto? _____ Semper fidelis _____

4. How do you say, "Repeat" in Latin? __ repetite _____

5. How do you say, "Goodbye, Teacher" (male) in Latin? __ Vale, Magister ____

Lesson 18 Questions

1. What is the most common verb in any language? _____ to be _____

2. What does the *to be* verb show? _____ existence _____

Translate

Check ✓ whether each verb is singular or plural.

1. estis _____ you (pl.) are _____   ☐ singular ☑ plural

2. es _____ you (s.) are _____   ☑ singular ☐ plural

3. sunt _____ they are _____   ☐ singular ☑ plural

4. sum _____ I am _____   ☑ singular ☐ plural

5. sumus _____ we are _____   ☐ singular ☑ plural

6. est _____ he, she, it is _____   ☑ singular ☐ plural

Notes

Speaking Latin --Listen to the Lesson 18 track on your Prima Latina CD--

☐ Say each vocabulary word and its meaning five times. Practice your pronunciation.

☐ Ask your family and friends, "How are you?" in Latin this week.

Write and Learn

1. Write each vocabulary word and its meaning twice.

1. _____   _____

   _____   _____

2. _____   _____

   _____   _____

3. _____   _____

   _____   _____

4. _____   _____

   _____   _____

5. _____   _____

   _____   _____

6. _____   _____

   _____   _____

Fun Practice

Find your favorite storybook. Read the first three pages and count how many times you see the *to be* verb in the present tense. Look for the words **is, am, are.**

Practical Latin

Satis bene   – very well

Lesson – To Be Able To / I Can

Sometimes we like to talk about the things we are **able to do**, the things we **can** do.

For instance, here are some of the things I **can** do:

I **can** swim.

I **am able to** ride a bike.

I **can** sing.

I **am able to** play the flute.

Other examples:

You **are able** to run.

He **is able** to ski.

She **can** ride horses.

We **are able** to hear.

They **are able** to dance.

* It is important not to confuse the word **can** with the word **may**.

Can is used when you are capable.

May is used when you are allowed.

In Latin there is a special **I can** verb.

Notice the similarities with the *to be* verb from Lesson 18.

Vocabulary

Here are the forms of **to be able to**.

1. pos**sum**	I can
2. pot**es**	you (s.) can
3. pot**est**	he, she, it can
4. pos**sumus**	we can
5. pot**estis**	you (pl.) can
6. pos**sunt**	they can

Latin Prayers (The Our Father or Lord's Prayer)

Fiat voluntas Tua   – Your will be done

Derivatives

possible   -- can be (adj.)

Review Questions

1. Practice saying the Doxology once from memory.

2. Write the Doxology once for practice.

Gloria Patri,

et Filio, et Spiritui Sancto.

Sicut erat in principio,

et nunc, et semper,

et in saecula saeculorum. Amen.

Lesson 19 Questions

1. What do all the *I can* verbs have in common? _____ they all begin with 'po' _____

2. What verb is present in all the *I can* verbs? they end in the "to be" verb endings

Translate

Check ✓ whether each verb is singular or plural.

1. possumus _____ we can _____ ☐ singular ✓plural

2. potestis _____ you (pl.) can _____ ☐ singular ✓plural

3. potes _____ you (s.) can _____ ✓singular ☐ plural

4. possum _____ I can _____ ✓singular ☐ plural

5. potest _____ he, she, it can _____ ✓singular ☐ plural

6. possunt _____ they can _____ ☐ singular ✓plural

Speaking Latin --Listen to the Lesson 19 track on your Prima Latina CD--

☐ Say each vocabulary word and its meaning five times. Practice your pronunciation.

☐ When people ask how you are this week, answer in Latin.

(And then in English to be polite.)

Write and Learn

1. Write each vocabulary word and its meaning twice.

1. _____   _____

    _____   _____

2. _____   _____

    _____   _____

3. _____   _____

    _____   _____

4. _____   _____

    _____   _____

5. _____   _____

    _____   _____

6. _____   _____

    _____   _____

Fun Practice

Make a list of 10 things you CAN do.

1. _____   6. _____

2. _____   7. _____

3. _____   8. _____

4. _____   9. _____

5. _____   10. _____

Practical Latin

Romanus civis sum   – I am a citizen of Rome

Lesson – Future Tense

Everything we have talked about so far has been in the **present tense**.
Present tense means that something is happening right now.

> For example:
>
> I learn. *OR*   I am learning.
>
> I sit. *OR* I am sitting.
>
> I write. *OR* I am writing.

Sometimes, there are things we look forward to happening in the **future**.
In English, we add the word *will* to indicate something will happen
in the **future**.

> For example:
>
> I <u>will</u> go on vacation this summer.
>
> I <u>will</u> graduate from high school in 10 years.
>
> I <u>will</u> go to the park tomorrow.

In Latin, instead of adding the extra word *will*, we add a special ending to our verbs.

On the following page are the **Future Tense Verb Endings.**
They are added to verbs, not used alone.
Again, notice the similarities with the other verb endings.

Grammar

Below are the future tense verb endings. They are added to verbs to form future tense. An example is voca**bo** - I will call.

Notice the highlighted endings.

1. b**o**	I will
2. bi**s**	you will
3. bi**t**	he, she, or it will
4. bi**mus**	we will
5. bi**tis**	you (pl.) will
6. bu**nt**	they will

Latin Prayers (The Our Father or Lord's Prayer)

Sicut in Caelo et in terra   – As in Heaven and on earth

Review Questions

1. What does a **J** sound like in Latin? _____ Y _____
2. What are the letters **A, E, I, O, U** called? _____ vowels _____
3. How many letters are in the Latin alphabet? _____ 25 _____
4. What does a Latin **E** sound like? _____ English long A (ay as in way)
5. What does a Latin **I** sound like? _____ English long E (ee as in see)

Lesson 20 Questions

1. What tense describes things that are happening right now? _____ present tense _____
2. What tense describes things that are going to happen? _____ future tense _____
3. What word do we add to sentences in English to show future tense? _____ will _____
4. How are future tense endings similar to all other verb endings we have learned? __
   _____ they end in "o, s, t, mus, tis, nt" _____

Speaking Latin   --Listen to the Lesson 20 track on your Prima Latina CD--

☐ Say each future tense verb ending and its meaning five times. Practice your pronunciation.

Notes

Write and Learn

1. Write each future tense ending and its meaning twice.

    1. _____   _____
        _____   _____

    2. _____   _____
        _____   _____

    3. _____   _____
        _____   _____

    4. _____   _____
        _____   _____

    5. _____   _____
        _____   _____

    6. _____   _____
        _____   _____

2. Write the Latin Prayers from Lessons 16 through 20, the Lord's Prayer, and translate.

    _____ Pater Noster, qui es in caelis, _____

    _____ sanctificetur nomen Tuum. _____

    _____ Adveniat regnum Tuum. _____

    _____ Fiat voluntas Tua, _____

    _____ sicut in Caelo et in terra. _____

Fun Practice

Write a list of ten things you will do in the future.

1. _____   6. _____
2. _____   7. _____
3. _____   8. _____
4. _____   9. _____
5. _____   10. _____

Vocabulary

Aquarius	water carrier
Aries	ram
Cancer	crab
Capricorn	goat
Gemini	twins
Virgo	maiden
Leo	lion
Libra	scales
Pisces	fish
Sagittarius	archer
Scorpio	scorpion
Taurus	bull

Grammar

To Be Verb

sum	I am
es	you are
est	he, she, it is
sumus	we are
estis	you (pl.) are
sunt	they are

To Be Able/Can Verb

possum	I can
potes	you can
potest	he, she, it can
possumus	we can
potestis	you (pl.) can
possunt	they can

Future Tense Endings

bo	I will
bis	you will
bit	he, she, it will
bimus	we will
bitis	you (pl.) will
bunt	they will

> **Latin Song**-- Refrain of
> "Resonet in Laudibus"
> Gaudete--Rejoice!
> Gaudete--Rejoice!

Practical Latin

Semper Fidelis	Always Faithful
repetite	repeat
Quid agis?	How are you?
Satis bene	very well
Romanus civis sum	I am a citizen of Rome

Latin Prayers (The Our Father or Lord's Prayer)

Pater Noster, qui es in caelis,	Our Father, who is in heaven,
sanctificetur nomen Tuum.	hallowed be Your name.
Adveniat regnum Tuum.	Your kingdom come.
Fiat voluntas Tua,	Your will be done,
sicut in Caelo et in terra.	on earth as it is in heaven.

A. *Copy all vocabulary words and translate.*

Extra: Write one derivative next to each word.

	Word	Derivative	Translation
1.	_____	_____	_____
2.	_____	_____	_____
3.	_____	_____	_____
4.	_____	_____	_____
5.	_____	_____	_____
6.	_____	_____	_____
7.	_____	_____	_____
8.	_____	_____	_____
9.	_____	_____	_____
10.	_____	_____	_____
11.	_____	_____	_____
12.	_____	_____	_____
13.	_____	_____	_____
14.	_____	_____	_____
15.	_____	_____	_____
16.	_____	_____	_____
17.	_____	_____	_____
18.	_____	_____	_____
19.	_____	_____	_____
20.	_____	_____	_____
21.	_____	_____	_____
22.	_____	_____	_____
23.	_____	_____	_____
24.	_____	_____	_____
25.	_____	_____	_____
26.	_____	_____	_____
27.	_____	_____	_____
28.	_____	_____	_____
29.	_____	_____	_____
30.	_____	_____	_____

B. Answer the following questions.

1. What are groups of stars in the sky called? ___constellations___

2. What is the most common verb? ___to be___

3. What tense describes things that *will* happen? ___future tense___

4. What tense describes things that are happening? ___present tense___

5. What is a word that names a specific person, place, or thing? ___proper noun___

6. What part of speech shows relationship and/or location? ___preposition___

7. What part of speech describes a noun or pronoun? ___adjective___

8. What part of speech describes a verb? ___adverb___

C. Practice saying the first half of the Lord's Prayer. Write it & translate.

Pater Noster, qui es in caelis,	Our Father, who is in heaven
sanctificetur nomen Tuum.	hallowed be Your name.
Adveniat regnum Tuum.	Your kingdom come.
Fiat voluntas Tua,	Your will be done,
sicut in Caelo et in terra.	on earth as it is in heaven.

D. Translate.

1. Always Faithful ___Semper fidelis___

2. Quid agis? ___How are you?___

3. nurturing mother ___alma mater___

4. wonder of the world ___stupor mundi___

5. Thanks be to God ___Deo gratias___

6. my fault ___mea culpa___

7. In the Year of our Lord ___Anno Domini___

8. Oremus ___Let us pray.___

E. Lingua Angelica Extra:

Sing the Refrain of, "Resonet in Laudibus" with the CD.
Write the Latin words once and translate.

_____

_____

_____

_____

_____

_____

Notes

_____

_____

_____

_____

_____

_____

_____

_____

_____

_____

_____

_____

_____

Practical Latin

E pluribus unum   – One out of many

Lesson – Conjunctions

Sicut, et, and sed, in today's vocabulary list are **conjunctions**.

A conjunction is a word that joins words or groups of words.

Examples:

I like to swim **and** I like to run.

You are in Latin **but** you are not in my class.

Forgive us our debts **as** we forgive our debtors.

Note: The words *etiam* and *non* are adverbs.

Vocabulary

1. sicut	as
2. et	and
3. sed	but
4. etiam	also
5. non	not

Latin Prayers (The Our Father or Lord's Prayer)

Panem nostrum cotidianum da nobis hodie

– Give us this day our daily bread.

Review Questions

1. What kind of word shows a relationship? <u>prepositions</u>

2. In what letter do all simple verbs end? <u>o</u>

3. In what letter do nouns in our first group end? <u>a</u>

4. What is the most important verb in any language? <u>to be</u>

5. What tense describes something that will happen? <u>future</u>

Lesson 21 Exercises

Write a sentence in English with each of the vocabulary words in Lesson 21.

1. _____

2. _____

3. _____

4. _____

5. _____

Translate

1. sed   <u>but</u>

2. sicut   <u>as</u>

3. non   <u>not</u>

4. etiam   <u>also</u>

5. et   <u>and</u>

Speaking Latin --Listen to the Lesson 21 track on your Prima Latina CD-- _____

☐ Say each vocabulary word and its meaning three times.

☐ Look for "E pluribus unum" on the dollar bill.

Say this Latin phrase each time you buy something.

Write and Learn _____

1. Write each vocabulary word and its meaning twice.

    1. _____   _____

       _____   _____

    2. _____   _____

       _____   _____

    3. _____   _____

       _____   _____

    4. _____   _____

       _____   _____

    5. _____   _____

       _____   _____

Fun Practice _____

Fill in the blanks.

1. I am as _____ strong _____, as _____ .

2. I am good at _____ , and also _____ .

3. I like _____ , but I don't like _____ .

4. I am not _____ .

5. I also like_____ .

Practical Latin

Ego amo te   – I love you.

Lesson - Question Words

We ask questions when we want to find out information - when we want an answer. The vocabulary for this lesson lists words that indicate a question in Latin.

We can recognize *question sentences* because they always have a **question mark.** A **question mark** looks like this: **?**

Examples:

Where are you going?

What school do you attend?

Why do you learn Latin?

Who is your teacher?

Vocabulary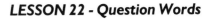

1. quis	who?
2. quid	what?
3. ubi	where?
4. cur	why?

Latin Prayers (The Our Father or Lord's Prayer)

Et dimitte nobis debita nostra   – and forgive us our debts

Derivatives

inquisitive	-- questioning (adj.)
ubiquitous	-- seemingly everywhere (adj.)
query	-- question (n.)
curious	-- eager to know (adj.)

Review Questions

1. Practice counting 1-10 out loud in Latin.

2. Write the numbers 1-10 in Latin.

   1. _____unus_____   6. _____sex_____
   2. _____duo_____   7. _____septem_____
   3. _____tres_____   8. _____octo_____
   4. _____quattuor_____   9. _____novem_____
   5. _____quinque_____   10. _____decem_____

3. What is the name for a group of stars that form a picture? _____constellation_____

4. What is an English word that has a sound and meaning similar to a Latin word?

   _____ derivative _____

5. How do you say, "One out of many" in Latin? _____E pluribus unum_____

Lesson 22 Questions

1. Why do you ask questions? _____To find out information_____

2. How can you tell if a sentence is a question? _____It ends in a ? (question mark)_____

3. How do you say, " I love you." in Latin? _____Ego amo te._____

Translate

1. ubi   _____where_____
2. cur   _____why_____
3. quis   _____who_____
4. quid   _____what_____

Speaking Latin --*Listen to the Lesson 22 track on your Prima Latina CD--*

☐ Say each vocabulary word and its meaning five times. Practice your pronunciation.

☐ This week, say, "I love you" in Latin to the people you care about.

Write and Learn

Write each vocabulary word and its meaning twice.

1. _____   _____
   _____   _____

2. _____   _____
   _____   _____

3. _____   _____
   _____   _____

4. _____   _____
   _____   _____

Fun Practice

Write down five questions you have. Make sure you use a *question mark* at the end of the sentence. Ask the questions to someone close to you to receive the information you want.

1. _____
2. _____
3. _____
4. _____
5. _____

Practical Latin

  Optime!   – Excellent!

Lesson – The First Declension

In life, we use groups to help us keep information straight.

  There are food groups (meats, dairy, grains, etc).

  There are animal groups (birds, mammals, fish, etc).

  There are even people groups (nations, cities, familes, friends).

There are also groups to help us keep Latin grammar straight.

> Verb groups are called **Conjugations.**
>
> Noun groups are called **Declensions.**

A **Declension** is a group of nouns that has the same or similar endings when declined. The most important thing to learn for now is that **declensions** go with **nouns** - people, places, or things.

There are only five declensions (or noun groups) in Latin.

On the next page the endings in the **First Declension Singular** are listed.

(Remember that singular means one, and the singular pronouns are I, you, he, she, it.)

By simply learning this list, you have made a big leap in Latin. We will explain declensions more next year as you progress in your Latin study.

Grammar

First Declension, Singular

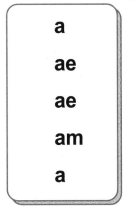

a
ae
ae
am
a

(ae has the long **A** sound)

Latin Prayers (The Our Father or Lord's Prayer)

Sicut et nos dimittimus debitoribus nostris
– As we also forgive our debtors.

Review Questions

1. Practice saying the first half of The Lord's Prayer from Lessons 16-20 plus what you have learned from Lessons 21-23. Write what you have learned from Lesson 21-23 once and translate it to English.

20

Panem nostrum cotidianum da nobis hodie,	Give us this day our daily bread,
et dimitte nobis debita nostra	and forgive us our debts
sicut et nos dimittimus debitoribus nostris.	as we also forgive our debtors.

21

Lesson 23 Questions

1. What is the name for a group of nouns with the same endings? __declension__

2. What kind of word does a declension go with? __a noun__

3. How many singular first declension endings are there? __five__

Speaking Latin --Listen to the Lesson 23 track on your *Prima Latina* CD--

☐ Say the first declension singular endings five times. Practice your pronunciation.

☐ When you do something well this week, say, "Excellent!" in Latin.

Write and Learn

Write the first declension singular endings three times.

a   _____ _____ _____

ae   _____ _____ _____

ae   _____ _____ _____

am   _____ _____ _____

a   _____ _____ _____

Fun Practice

Think of a poem or song to help you remember the first declension singular endings.

Practical Latin

Pessime!   – Very bad

Lesson – Declensions

Below is a list of the **First Declension Plural** endings.

(Remember *Plural* means more than one.)

Again, practice these from memory and watch your pronunciations.

Grammar

(Remember, **I** sounds like a long **E** in Latin.)

First Declension Plural Endings

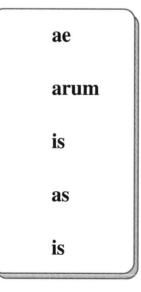

ae

arum

is

as

is

You have now learned the endings for the entire First Declension. Congratulations!

Latin Prayers (The Our Father or Lord's Prayer)

Et ne nos inducas in tentationem   – And lead us not into temptation

Review Questions

1. What does an **E** sound like in Latin? _____ English long A (ay as in way)
2. What does an **I** sound like in Latin? _____ English long E (ee as in see)
3. How do you say, "Repeat" in Latin? _____ Repetite.
4. How do you say, "Goodbye, friends" in Latin? _____ Valete, amici
5. How many vowels are in the Latin alphabet? _____ 5

Lesson 24 Questions

1. What does "plural" mean? _____ more than one
2. What kind of word goes with declensions? _a noun
3. How many first declension plural endings are there? _____ 5

Speaking Latin --Listen to the Lesson 24 track on your Prima Latina CD--

☐ Say the first declension plural endings five times. Practice your pronunciation.
☐ When you mess up this week say, "Pessime!"

Write and Learn

Write the first declension plural endings five times.

1. _____ ae
2. _____ arum
3. _____ is
4. _____ as
5. _____ is

Fun Practice

Add a line or verse to your poem or song from Lesson 23 to help you remember the first declension plural endings.

Practical Latin

Finis! – The End!

Lesson - First Conjugation

As you know, conjugations are verb groups.

Conjugating means changing a verb based on *who* or *what* is doing the action and *when* that action actually occurs.

Example: Think of the word *walk.*

If you are talking about yourself, you say: "I *walk.*"

If you are talking about your friend John, you say: "John *walks.*"

See how you change (or **conjugate**) the verb because of *who* is doing the verb.

Let's do another one. The verb is *run.*

If your dog, Spot, runs, you say: "Spot *runs.*"

If you run, you say: "I *run.*"

If you run with your dog, you say: "We *run.*"

A verb is also changed (or **conjugated**) because of *when* the verb happens. Look at the example below.

The verb is *call.*

If you called yesterday, you would say: "Yesterday I *called.*"

If you are going to call tomorrow, you say: "Tomorrow I *will call.*"

If you are calling right now, you say: "I *call.*"

For now, the most important thing to remember is that **conjugations** go with **verbs.**
We will talk more about **conjugations** as we learn more about the Latin language.

Grammar

These first conjugation verb endings are the pronoun letters from Lesson 13.

1. am**o**	I love
2. ama**s**	you love
3. ama**t**	he, she, it loves
4. ama**mus**	we love
5. ama**tis**	you (pl.) love
6. ama**nt**	they love

Latin Prayers (The Our Father or Lord's Prayer)

Sed libera nos a malo. Amen.   – But deliver us from evil. Amen.

Review Questions

1. What is an action word called? _____ verb _____

2. What kind of word modifies a verb? _____ adverb _____

3. What kind of word modifies a noun or pronoun? _____ adjective _____

4. What comes at the end of all question sentences? _____ ? (question mark) _____

5. What kind of word does "declension" go with? _____ noun _____

Lesson 25 Questions

1. What kind of word does "conjugation" go with? _____ verb _____

2. What are two things that cause a verb to change or be conjugated? _____
   _____ who or what does it & when it happens. _____

Translate

1. amas _____ you (s.) love _____

2. amo _____ I love _____

3. amamus _____ we love _____

4. amatis _____ you (pl.) love _____

5. amant _____ they love _____

6. amat _____ he, she, it loves _____

Speaking Latin --Listen to the Lesson 25 track on your Prima Latina CD--

☐ Say the first conjugation of "I love" five times. Practice your pronunciation.

☐ When you finish something this week, say, "Finis!"

Write and Learn

Write the first conjugation of "I love" three times in Latin.

amo	amo	amo
amas	amas	amas
amat	amat	amat
amamus	amamus	amamus
amatis	amatis	amatis
amant	amant	amant

Fun Practice

Draw a picture of a train with six cars. Put one form of "I love" in Latin in each car.

Be sure to put them in the order they are presented on the previous page.

Decorate your train any way you like.

Make a great caboose because you just ended your first year of Latin!

Vocabulary

Other Words

sicut — as
et — and
sed — but
etiam — also
non — not

Question Words

quis — who?
quid — what?
ubi — where?
cur — why?

First Declension Singular

a
ae
ae
am
a

First Declension Plural

ae
arum
is
as
is

First Conjugation

amo — I love
amas — you love
amat — he, she, it loves
amamus — we love
amatis — you (pl.) love
amant — they love

> **Latin Song**-- More of the Refrain of "Resonet in Laudibus"
>   Christus natus hodie--
>   Christ is born today

Practical Latin

E pluribus unum — One out of many
Ego amo te. — I love you.
Optime! — Excellent!
Pessime! — Very bad!
Finis — The end!

Sayings and Prayers (The Lord's Prayer or Our Father)

Panem nostrum cotidianum da nobis hodie,
et dimitte nobis debita nostra
sicut et nos dimittimus debitoribus nostris.
Et ne nos inducas in tentationem,
sed libera nos a malo. Amen.

Give us this day our daily bread,
and forgive us our debts
as we also forgive our debtors.
And lead us not into temptation,
but deliver us from evil. Amen.

A. Copy all vocabulary words and translate.

Extra: Write one derivative next to each word.

	Word	Derivative	Translation
1.	_____	_____	_____
2.	_____	_____	_____
3.	_____	_____	_____
4.	_____	_____	_____
5.	_____	_____	_____
6.	_____	_____	_____
7.	_____	_____	_____
8.	_____	_____	_____
9.	_____	_____	_____

B. Answer the following questions.

1. What kind of word does **declension** go with? _____ noun _____

2. What kind of word does **conjugation** go with? _____ verb _____

3. What goes at the end of all question sentences? _____ ? (question mark) _____

4. What are two reasons why you would conjugate a verb in a sentence? _____

_____ who or what does it changes, or when it happens changes _____

C. Review the entire Lord's Prayer below. When you are ready, cover the prayer, write it once completely, and translate into English.

Pater Noster, qui es in caelis,
sanctificetur nomen Tuum.
Adveniat regnum Tuum.
Fiat voluntas Tua,
sicut in Caelo et in terra.
Panem nostrum cotidianum da nobis hodie,
et dimitte nobis debita nostra
sicut et nos dimittimus debitoribus nostris.
Et ne nos inducas in tentationem,
sed libera nos a malo. Amen.

Our Father, who is in heaven,
hallowed be Your name.
Your kingdom come.
Your will be done,
on earth as it is in heaven.
Give us this day our daily bread,
and forgive us our debts
as we also forgive our debtors.
And lead us not into temptation,
but deliver us from evil. Amen.

D. Translate into Latin.

1. One out of many   E pluribus unum

2. I love you.   Ego amo te.

3. Excellent!   Optime!

4. Very bad!   Pessime!

5. The end!   Finis!

E. Lingua Angelica Extra:

Sing more of the Refrain of "Resonet in Laudibus."
Write the Latin words once and translate.

_____

_____

_____

_____

_____

_____

Notes

Appendix

VOCABULARY APPENDIX - ALPHABETICAL

adoro	*I adore*	verb (4)
altus	*high, deep*	adjective (14)
ambulo	*I walk*	verb (1)
amo	*I love*	verb (4)
aqua	*water*	noun (7)
aquarius	*water carrier*	noun (16)
aries	*ram*	noun (16)
bimus	*we will*	verb ending (20)
bis	*you will*	vern ending (20)
bit	*he, she, it will*	verb ending (20)
bitis	*you will*	verb ending (20)
bo	*I will*	verb ending (20)
bonus	*good*	adjective (14)
bunt	*they will*	verb ending (20)
caelum	*heaven*	noun (2)
cancer	*crab*	noun (16)
capricorn	*goat*	noun (16)
cena	*dinner*	noun (7)
clam	*secretly*	adverb (15)
clamo	*I shout*	verb (2)
contra	*against*	preposition (12)
corona	*crown*	noun (7)
cur	*why*	adverb (22)
decem	*ten*	adjective (10)
Deus	*God*	proper noun (1)
duo	*two*	adjective (9)
es	*you are*	verb (18)
est	*he, she, it is*	verb (18)
estis	*you are*	verb (18)
et	*and*	conjunction (21)
etiam	*also*	adverb (21)
ex	*out of*	preposition (12)
femina	*woman*	noun (8)
fortuna	*luck*	noun (8)
geminus	*twin*	noun (16)
gloria	*glory*	noun (2)
habito	*I live in*	verb (4)
herba	*herb*	noun (8)
Hispania	*Spain*	proper noun (11)
injuria	*injury*	noun (8)
inter	*between*	preposition (12)
Italia	*Italy*	proper noun (11)
Jesus	*Jesus*	proper noun (2)
judico	*I judge*	verb (4)
laboro	*I work*	verb (3)
laudo	*I praise*	verb (2)
leo	*lion*	noun (17)
libero	*I free*	verb (5)
libra	*scales*	noun (17)
longus	*long*	adjective (14)
luna	*moon*	noun (1)
Marcus	*Marcus*	proper noun (11)
Maria	*Mary*	proper noun (11)
mensa	*table*	noun (7)
multus	*much, many*	adjective (14)
narro	*I tell*	verb (5)
nauta	*sailor*	noun (8)
navigo	*I sail*	verb (3)
non	*not*	adverb (21)
novem	*nine*	adjective (10)
novus	*new*	adjective (14)
numquam	*never*	adverb (15)
nunc	*now*	adverb (15)
octo	*eight*	adjective (10)
oro	*I pray*	verb (3)
paro	*I prepare*	verb (4)
patria	*country*	noun (7)
pisces	*fish*	noun (17)
porto	*I carry*	verb (3)
possum	*I can*	verb (19)
possumus	*we can*	verb (19)
possunt	*they can*	verb (19)
potes	*you can*	verb (19)
potest	*he, she, it can*	verb (19)
potestis	*you can*	verb (19)
pugno	*I fight*	verb (5)
quattuor	*four*	adjective (9)
quid	*what*	adverb (22)
quinque	*five*	adjective (9)
quis	*who*	pronoun (22)
regina	*queen*	noun (6)
Roma	*Rome*	proper noun (11)
saepe	*often*	adverb (15)
sagittarius	*archer*	noun (17)
scorpio	*scorpion*	noun (17)
sed	*but*	conjunction (21)
semper	*always*	adverb (15)
septem	*seven*	adjective (10)
sex	*six*	adjective (10)
sicut	*as*	adverb (21)
silva	*forest*	noun (6)
specto	*I look at*	verb (3)
stella	*star*	noun (6)
sub	*under*	preposition (12)
sum	*I am*	verb (18)
sumus	*we are*	verb (18)
sunt	*they are*	verb (18)
supero	*I conquer*	verb (5)
supra	*above*	preposition (12)
taurus	*bull*	noun (17)
terra	*earth*	noun (6)
toga	*toga*	noun (1)
tres	*three*	adjective (9)
ubi	*where*	adverb (22)
unda	*wave*	noun (6)
unus	*one*	adjective (9)
via	*road*	noun (1)
virgo	*maiden, virgin*	noun (16)
vita	*life*	noun (6)
voco	*I call*	verb (5)

altus	*high, deep*	adjective (14)
bonus	*good*	adjective (14)
decem	*ten*	adjective (10)
duo	*two*	adjective (9)
longus	*long*	adjective (14)
multus	*much, many*	adjective (14)
novem	*nine*	adjective (10)
novus	*new*	adjective (14)
octo	*eight*	adjective (10)
quattuor	*four*	adjective (9)
quinque	*five*	adjective (9)
septem	*seven*	adjective (10)
sex	*six*	adjective (10)
tres	*three*	adjective (9)
unus	*one*	adjective (9)
clam	*secretly*	adverb (15)
cur	*why*	adverb (22)
etiam	*also*	adverb (21)
non	*not*	adverb (21)
numquam	*never*	adverb (15)
nunc	*now*	adverb (15)
quid	*what*	adverb (22)
saepe	*often*	adverb (15)
semper	*always*	adverb (15)
sicut	*as*	adverb (21)
ubi	*where*	adverb (22)
et	*and*	conjunction (21)
sed	*but*	conjunction (21)
aqua	*water*	noun (7)
aquarius	*water carrier*	noun (16)
aries	*ram*	noun (16)
caelum	*heaven*	noun (2)
cancer	*crab*	noun (16)
capricorn	*goat*	noun (16)
cena	*dinner*	noun (7)
corona	*crown*	noun (7)
femina	*woman*	noun (8)
fortuna	*luck*	noun (8)
geminus	*twin*	noun (16)
gloria	*glory*	noun (2)
herba	*herb*	noun (8)
injuria	*injury*	noun (8)
leo	*lion*	noun (17)
libra	*scales*	noun (17)
luna	*moon*	noun (1)
mensa	*table*	noun (7)
nauta	*sailor*	noun (8)
patria	*country*	noun (7)
pisces	*fish*	noun (17)
regina	*queen*	noun (6)
sagittarius	*archer*	noun (17)
scorpio	*scorpion*	noun (17)
silva	*forest*	noun (6)
stella	*star*	noun (6)
taurus	*bull*	noun (17)
terra	*earth*	noun (6)
toga	*toga*	noun (1)
unda	*wave*	noun (6)
via	*road*	noun (1)
virgo	*maiden, virgin*	noun (16)
vita	*life*	noun (6)
contra	*against*	preposition (12)
ex	*out of*	preposition (12)
inter	*between*	preposition (12)
sub	*under*	preposition (12)
supra	*above*	preposition (12)
quis	*who*	pronoun (22)
Deus	*God*	proper noun (1)
Hispania	*Spain*	proper noun (11)
Italia	*Italy*	proper noun (11)
Jesus	*Jesus*	proper noun (2)
Marcus	*Marcus*	proper noun (11)
Maria	*Mary*	proper noun (11)
Roma	*Rome*	proper noun (11)
adoro	*I adore*	verb (4)
ambulo	*I walk*	verb (1)
amo	*I love*	verb (4)
clamo	*I shout*	verb (2)
es	*you are*	verb (18)
est	*he, she, it is*	verb (18)
estis	*you are*	verb (18)
habito	*I live in*	verb (4)
judico	*I judge*	verb (4)
laboro	*I work*	verb (3)
laudo	*I praise*	verb (2)
libero	*I free*	verb (5)
narro	*I tell*	verb (5)
navigo	*I sail*	verb (3)
oro	*I pray*	verb (3)
paro	*I prepare*	verb (4)
porto	*I carry*	verb (3)
possum	*I can*	verb (19)
possumus	*we can*	verb (19)
possunt	*they can*	verb (19)
potes	*you can*	verb (19)
potest	*he, she, it can*	verb (19)
potestis	*you can*	verb (19)
pugno	*I fight*	verb (5)
specto	*I look at*	verb (3)
sum	*I am*	verb (18)
sumus	*we are*	verb (18)
sunt	*they are*	verb (18)
supero	*I conquer*	verb (5)
voco	*I call*	verb (5)
bimus	*we will*	verb ending (20)
bit	*he, she, it will*	verb ending (20)
bitis	*you will*	verb ending (20)
bo	*I will*	verb ending (20)
bunt	*they will*	verb ending (20)
bis	*you will*	vern ending (20)

Lesson	Practical Latin	Translation
1	Salve!	– Hello! (to one person)
	Salvete!	– Hello! (to more than one person)
2	Magister	– Teacher (male)
	Magistra	– Teacher (female)
3	Surge	– Stand up (one person)
	Surgite	– Stand up (more than one person)
4	Vale	– Goodbye (to one person)
	Valete	– Goodbye (to more than one person)
5	Discipulus	– student
	Discipuli	– students
	(sc has a 'sh' sound)	
6	Deo Gratias	– Thanks be to God
7	Mea Culpa	– my fault
8	amicus	– friend
	amici	– friends
9	Sedete	– Sit Down (to many)
10	Anno Domini, A.D.	– In the Year of our Lord
11	Veni, vidi, vici	– I came, I saw, I conquered. (Julius Caesar)
12	Quo vadis?	– Where are you going?
13	alma mater	– nurturing mother
14	Stupor Mundi	– wonder of the world
15	Nunc aut numquam	– Now or never
16	Semper Fidelis	– Always Faithful (Marine Corps motto)
17	Repetite	– Repeat (to many)
18	Quid agis?	– How are you?
19	Satis bene	– very well
20	Romanus civis sum	– I am a citizen of Rome
21	E pluribus unum	– One out of many
22	Ego amo te	– I love you.
23	Optime!	– Excellent!
24	Pessime!	– Very bad
25	Finis!	– The End!